SIGHT-FISHING THE FLATS AND BEYOND

Captain Nick Karas

STACKPOLE
BOOKS

0 11557 03465 3

Published by
STACKPOLE BOOKS
5067 Ritter Road
Mechanicsburg, PA 17055
www.stackpolebooks.com

Printed in China

First edition

10 9 8 7 6 5 4 3 2 1

Cover design by Wendy A. Reynolds

Cover photograph by Nick Karas

All photographs by the author or Shirley Karas except on page 26 (top): Ron Modra; and pages 45, 98, 99: Paul Bereswell

All fish illustrations by Duane Raver except on page 3 (striped bass), 25 (permit), and 35 (bonefish): Flick Ford

Library of Congress Cataloging-in-Publication Data

Karas, Nick.
  Sight-fishing the flats and beyond / Nick Karas.
      p. cm.
  Includes index.
  ISBN-13: 978-0-8117-3465-3
  ISBN-10: 0-8117-3465-X
  1. Saltwater fishing. I. Title.

SH457.3.K37 2008
799.16—dc22
                                                          2007017527

CONTENTS

To my wife, Shirl, who ran a trotline before I ever tasted salt

INTRODUCTION

In the minds of many nonanglers and even some anglers, fishing is just one jerk on the end of a line waiting for a jerk on the other. This may be true of some fishers, but it isn't necessarily so if you become a fish hunter. A fish hunter aggressively seeks out fish instead of waiting for them to assault the lure or bait. In a real sense, this kind of angler becomes a predator, in many ways resembling the fish he or she is seeking, because this type of fishing works only on predatory fish.

Sight fishing, also called finesse fishing or fish hunting, is at the cutting edge of recreational fishing's rapid expansion in the marine environment. It is here where real innovations in fishing technique are occurring almost daily. The basic philosophy shared by all sight-fishing anglers is that what you catch is less important than how you catch it.

The concept of sight fishing probably originated in Florida's mangrove "forests," a coastal perimeter that surrounds the Sunshine State from St. Augustine south to the Florida Keys, then north along the Gulf coast to Pensacola. These chlorophyllous inhabitants of a mangal—a community of compatible subtropical and tropical plant species—include both bushes and trees that readily take root in depositional marine, tidal, and coastal environments. These areas, which contain fine sediment with a high organic content, are protected from the brunt force of waves by barrier beaches. The mangal plants develop an elaborate root system in the spaces between the sand or mud bottoms and the high-tide water level. What is important to anglers about these groves is that their roots are inhabited by snook, a genuine predator fish that makes sight-fishing possible.

Hunting the mangroves for snook with bait quickly became popular among local Floridian fishermen. Some even began hunting them with lures and flies. The thrill of fishing the mangroves was eventually discovered by fly rod–toting northerners trying to escape the cold and hoping to extend their fishing season. Upon returning north, these anglers began searching for predator fishing on their home turf. Although mangroves don't grow north of Florida because of their susceptibility to frost, northerly haunts composed of vast stands of sedges and phragmites house a variety of other predator fish that can be taken by the same fish-hunting techniques on the flats and back bays.

The basic sight-fishing scenario is one in which you see a fish before you catch it. It is an effort whereby one predator (the angler) is chasing a half dozen other predators (the fish). In the Northeast, these predator fish might be striped bass, bluefish, bonito, albacore, weakfish, or fluke (summer flounder). In the southeastern Atlantic, around the southern tip of Florida, and as far west as Texas, you'll find sea trout, bluefish, redfish, jack crevalle, barracuda, ladyfish, snook, permit, bonefish, and tarpon. In all, there are sixteen species of fish that haunt the shallow tidal flats in search of food.

Some practitioners like to describe the sport as fish hunting, because stalking the fish closely parallels the experience of stalking a deer, with a fly rod (or, in some cases, a spinning rod) taking the place of a rifle or bow. But whereas deer hunters use their senses of hearing and sometimes smell, eyesight dominates the fish-hunting game. The adrenaline rush upon sighting the prey is incomparable to any other fishing experience, but it produces a high that is equivalent in some respects to buck fever. I have seen anglers on the bow platform of a boat suddenly freeze at the sight of a dozen 15- to 20-pound striped bass casually swimming in their direction, moving unhurriedly under the bow of the boat, and swimming out the other side in just 3 feet of crystal clear water.

Searching the flats for fish movement requires intense concentration by both the angler and the navigator.

PART I

The Fish

It has been alleged that sometime during the fourth century, as a Roman army was poised on the north side of the Alps, preparing to oppose a mob of attacking Germanic tribes, a young centurion approached his commander and asked, "How, Sir, should we repulse their attack?" The general paused for a moment, then responded, "Know thine enemy and he is yours." Obviously, neither the general nor his subordinate knew much about the invading barbarians because they lost the battle and were driven south, and so began the decline of the Roman Empire.

Although the stakes in sight fishing are not quite as high, there is much that sight fishers can learn from this advice. If you really know the habits of the fish you are seeking—how, when, and where it feeds, and what it likes to eat— your chances of catching it are vastly improved. This is especially true for predator fish. This book will help you get to know thy fish without even getting your feet wet. In addition, there are scores of books available on almost

Wading and casting from shore can produce fish, but nothing in comparison to what an angler with a boat can do.

every species of fish, magazine articles dedicated strictly to these fish, and the Internet. Reading, digesting, and assimilating all this information is the first step.

The next step is getting out and doing the field-work, which can be accomplished in one of two ways. The first way is to learn from someone who has already been infected by the sight-fishing bug. If you can't find an angler with a boat who's willing to take you out for free, hire a guide who specializes in sight fishing and learn from an expert. The second approach is to gradually learn on your own, but this can be a slow process. Again, use this book to guide you.

WHAT ARE PREDATOR FISH?

Predator fish are those that overtly seek other fish or marine animals with some degree of mobility and aggressively chase and feed on them. A predator fish is one that uses all its senses—sight, smell, taste, and hearing—to catch its meal. Paramount among these four senses is sight. In most instances, sight is the first sense that locates the prey, allowing the predator to actively seek and attack its prey. Some predator fish can continue feeding into the night. Though their sight is diminished, they can use sound to help locate prey. Fish have no exposed eardrums, but they do have a subcutaneous line of sensory organs (neuromasts) located along each side of their body that closely follows their lateral lines. These very sensitive organs allow fish to feel or hear sounds made by other fish. Taste and smell can be long-distance guides to locating food, but they are used primarily to lead the predator near to the victim; then sight takes over.

WHERE ARE PREDATOR FISH FOUND?

Three marine sight-fishing environments exist where the techniques described in this book can be effective in catching predatory fish: inshore, nearshore, and blue water. These environments differ in two ways: water depth where fishing takes places, and distance from shore, be it an island or the mainland.

Inshore fishing takes place along the immediate shoreline, both outside and inside barrier beaches and in sounds, bays, deltas, and tidal estuaries. Here, anglers fish from shore, using wading to expand their range. Of the three sight-fishing environments, fishing from shore is the least effective. Although fishing from the beach is easy and fun, keeping your feet stuck in the sand and being limited in range by your casting ability can greatly reduce the scope of your fishing realm.

The nearshore environment is composed of the same basic conditions that prevail when fishing inshore, but angling is done from a small boat. The same waters are fished, but from the outside in. In addition, boat-equipped anglers can venture farther offshore among islands or around points of land with relatively deeper water around them. With the mobility of a boat, anglers can cover more water and even follow fish as they move about. Of the three environments, this one is fished most often and is most productive.

The so-called blue-water environment is an area that extends seaward from the barrier beaches into deeper water. Here, fish are sought on shoals that rise from deeper water or around islands or the waters between them and the mainland. (True blue-water fishing involves big-game fishing farther offshore in the deep waters over the continental shelf and its canyons. This is not sight fishing, because even though anglers might be casting to a school of fish on the surface, they are dependent on random or unexpected encounters with fish or utilize chumming to draw fish to the boat. Fishing for these true blue-water predators is done from large boats capable of safely venturing as much as 70 miles offshore.)

More than two dozen species of fish are available to sight fishers; however, not all species are found in the same waters. These waters can be roughly divided into six areas: (1) along the Atlantic coast from Maine to the Cape Hatteras, North Carolina; (2) from Hatteras south to the tip of Florida; (3) the Gulf of Mexico from the southern tip of Florida, north along the coast to Texas, and on to southern Mexico; (4) the coast of Central America and the Caribbean, across central and northern South America to the heel of Brazil; (5) the Bahamas and the Windward and Leeward islands of the Caribbean Sea; and (6) Bermuda, where serious bonefishing began.

Even within these areas, conditions can vary, and pigeonholing which fish species are found where is not easy. Some migrate only short distances from their summer and winter waters, and others make a grand swim that is well over 1,000 miles. In general, in inshore and nearshore environments in the northeastern Atlantic, predator fish are more prone to migrate. They spend spring to fall in shallow-water bays and estuaries or within a few miles of the beaches. The rest of the year, they are found in the southern part of their range, and some may travel as far as the Florida coast. In the Southeast and Gulf of Mexico, predator species are available in all three environments throughout the year, but even here, there is some southward-northward coastal movement with the seasons.

CHAPTER 1

Atlantic Inshore Species

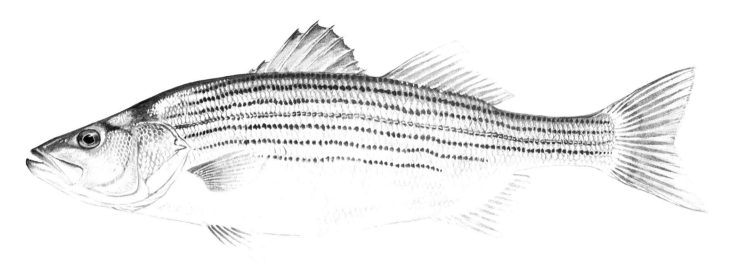

Striped bass (*Morone saxatilis*)

STRIPED BASS (*Morone saxatilis*)

Regardless of what fishing techniques you employ, the striped bass is the number-one gamefish along the Atlantic coast from Maine to northern Florida, although they are most numerous from Cape Cod to Cape Hatteras. Unlike the other fish you might encounter in marine waters, striped bass are freshwater fish that have evolved a unique kidney, giving them the ability to swim in either fresh or salt water. However, to reproduce successfully, they must spawn in fresh water.

Striped bass are the perfect prey for sight-fishing anglers because they are schooling fish that prefer the inshore habitat. Almost the only time they are found in blue water is when they are migrating, crossing from one point of land to the next. The exception is when many of the large spawners, primarily bass originating from the Potomac River, winter over in deep water offshore, 30 to 40 miles east of the Virginia–North Carolina border.

The majority of striped bass tend to inhabit marine estuarine environments, primarily from spring to fall. Contrary to what many anglers believe, the general populations of striped bass are not highly migratory fish. Most make short, seasonal food migrations down their freshwater rivers to the estuary and bracket each side of

the bay in a saline environment. In addition, there may be short seasonal migrations into salt water based on rising water temperatures in the river. The exceptions to these migration patterns are striped bass populations spawned in the Potomac River, a major river entering the northwest corner of Chesapeake Bay, and in a few associated rivers nearby. After the Chesapeake and Delaware Canal was enlarged for oceangoing vessels in the early 1920s, these fish developed a proclivity to wander north out of Chesapeake Bay into Delaware Bay. From Delaware Bay they head north along the coast to summer in the waters between Montauk Point, Long Island, and Buzzards Bay, Massachusetts. Reverse migration occurs in the fall.

Striped bass production from the Potomac and associated rivers is so great that for nearly a century it overshadowed the more typical life cycles of fish produced in other coastal rivers from the St. Lawrence to the St. Johns River in northern Florida. It wasn't until an extensive tag-and-release program was inaugurated by a New Jersey brewery, involving the voluntary efforts of hundreds of recreational anglers, that the river origins of striped bass along the Northeast coast were finally determined.

From late spring to early fall in the Northeast, striped bass are hunted by sight fishers in two environments—the flats and the mini-flats located immediately adjacent to the true flats. During early spring, after spawning, striped bass migrate north along the Atlantic coast and are most vulnerable off beaches associated with flats. In late fall, the opposite direction is in play. When spring waters get too warm for bass, the fish move off the flats. This is the beginning of the mini-flats or structure-fishing phase, involving deeper waters off points of land and around islands. Here, the flats are usually narrow and quickly drop into deeper, cooler waters. The fish move onto the flats to feed late in the day, throughout the night, and for an hour or so after sunrise. In late July and August, when water temperatures on the flats and even on the structures rise above 70 degrees, bass stay in even deeper, cooler waters. They usually approach the shoals to feed only on a flooding tide that comes in from the cooler ocean.

As noted, striped bass are temperature sensitive. The majority of their feeding takes place in water temperatures ranging from 60 to 69 degrees. This becomes crucial when fishing on the flats. Bass are attracted to these shallow-water habitats in early spring because they follow their food. However, when water temperatures reach 70 degrees, they avoid these flats because water 71 degrees and warmer can be lethal to large bass. Smaller bass can withstand water temperatures a few degrees higher, but not for long. Conversely, when water temperatures drop below 50 degrees, striped bass become lethargic and seldom feed. This is especially true at the tidal mouths of streams and rivers, which the bass will ascend in the spring to spawn. If the estuary has relatively deep water, striped bass may use this environment to winter over, even though it may be ice covered.

Fly-Fishing for Striped Bass

Rods. The best weight rod to use when fly-fishing for bass on the flats is a 9–10-weight rod with a fast tip and a butt extension. This combination-weight rod is ideal, because you never know how large a bass you might run into. There have been times when I've watched a school of more than 100 fish, all 8- to 12-pounders, swim past the bow of my flats boat. Then a few miles farther down the flats I've run into another school of bass, but this time, they were all 18- to 20-pounders. And still farther on, another school might be all 5- to 7-pound fish. The reason for this variety in weights is that striped bass often school by year classes. That is, all the fish produced in one year seem to stay together in subsequent years. The 9–10-weight rod won't overpower the smaller bass but will give you a good chance of landing a 25-pounder if

that school comes along. Bass may school in large numbers on the flats, but an average school is usually composed of two to three dozen fish. But note this rule of thumb: the larger the fish, the smaller the school.

Lines. Floating lines with weighted-forward tapers work best most of the time. If you delight in throwing a popper or a bug or a large fly in 2 to 3 feet of water, you might opt for the same line with a shorter taper. This allows the line to turn over more easily, especially if you're casting into the wind. You can even buy a saltwater taper that is shorter than a bug or rocket taper. If you are working the edge of a flat, following the tide as it rises and floods the flat (see chapter 16), you might want to have another rod handy, again loaded with a floating line but with a sinking tip. The heavier tip gets the fly into deeper water, where the bass are likely to be watching.

Leaders. If you plan to fish the flats with a guide, he or she will ask you to come prepared with 10- to 12-foot tapered leaders. The longer the leader, the more difficult it is to cast accurately, and accuracy is vital when casting to striped bass. I usually use heavy leaders, 15- to 20-pound-test, but cut the distal end short, down to 6 to 8 feet long. I like the heavier butt section of these heavy leaders because they make casting a bit easier. To compensate for the shorter leader, I use longer tippets, usually 4 to 5 feet long and always constructed of fluorocarbon. To the distal end of the tippet I use a clinch knot to tie on the lightest snap I can find. The snap allows you to change flies quickly, and it won't deter a fish from gulping the fly.

Flies. Striped bass are not difficult fish to catch, but because they have such a varied diet, it can be difficult to decide what lures to feed them. Despite being omnivorous eaters, bass have a penchant for feeding on only one kind of food at a time. The trick to catching them is to discover what is on their menu at the moment.

Because bass dine on such a wide variety of foods, ranging from small crustaceans and sand fleas to full-grown bunker, the size of bass flies and hooks can vary greatly. In general, small flies catch a lot of bass, but bigger flies seem to catch many more. Sizes can range from 1 to 4/0 and everything in between. Probably the most commonly used up-flies (so called because the curve of the hook is always up and clear of the bottom) are Clouser Minnows on size 1 to 4 hooks in brown and white, white and gold, or tan and gold. The white is always on the bottom of the fly. These flies are effective because bass do a lot of feeding in the mud or sand.

The most popular down-flies (hooks turned down) are the Deceivers, in sizes similar to the Clousers and in blue and white, yellow and white, green and white, or tan and white. Not to be outdone are Crazy Charlies,

Deciding which fly will work is not always a choice when omnivorous striped bass are involved.

flies designed especially for bonefish but loved by rooting bass. Big bunker or mullet flies with large eyes also make any bass lust for a bite. As good as any bass flies are the various sizes of Blados Crease flies. Add to this collection almost any shrimp or crab pattern, and you will be prepared with just about every fly bass will devour.

Spin-Fishing for Striped Bass

Because all sizes of striped bass, from 6- to 30-pounders, swim onto the flats in search of food, one spinning outfit is usually not enough—unless your flats are frequented only by bass of a certain size.

Rods. Regardless of the fish's size, the two or three rods needed to complete a striped bass spinning outfit should all possess the same basic characteristics. When sight-fishing on the flats, where you can't afford to let a bass have its way if the edges are cluttered with snags, boulders, or tall grasses, the rod must have some beef to it, even if the fish are only 3 to 6 pounds. Pick a $7^{1}/_{2}$-foot graphite rod with ceramic inserts in the first and second ring guides, a saltwater-proof reel seat, and a blank rated to handle 8- to 12-pound-test lines and light- to medium-weight plugs. For all rods, a stiff or fast tip is a must, for two reasons: to help you cast light lures farther, and to help you control where the bass can swim.

For progressively larger bass, the rod length should be increased by a half foot or a foot, the rod handle can be a bit longer, and the reel size should be increased to hold slightly stronger line as well as more of it. The incremental changes between the rods shouldn't be too drastic—just a slightly bigger version to match a bigger fish.

Reels. Striped bass don't make blitzing runs like bonefish or permit do. Instead, a 100-foot dash is usually all they can muster. Their forte is their strength. At the end of the run, they stop and act like bulldogs refusing to come in peacefully. Although larger reels allow you to load them with heavier lines, the drag system is most important when deciding which reel to pick. A smooth, easily adjusted drag is what you want.

Lines. Anglers who have developed a certain prowess when it comes to fighting striped bass on the flats pick lighter-test lines than do those new to this kind of fishing. For smaller bass, 6- to 8-pound-test monofilament or braided lines are used. If you are in new waters and have no idea what size fish to expect, opt for a reel loaded with 10- to 12- or 12- to 15-pound-test lines. If you know that the bass on your flats are in the 15- to 30-pound range, pick 15- to 18-pound-test lines. Even in these heavyweight classes, you can still use light lures if you choose fluorocarbon monofilament lines or

This bass fell for a noisy popper.

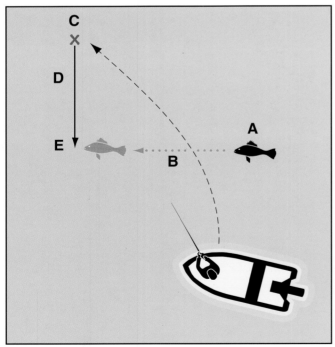

After spotting the bass, determine which direction it is heading, then drop a 2¹/₂- or 3¹/₂-inch popping plug about 10 feet past the fish and about the same distance ahead of where the bass is likely to be when you begin to retrieve the lure. After the lure lands, make one or two short yanks to get the fish's attention, then stop.

braided lines whose small diameter belies their real strength.

Lures. Striped bass are not supposed to jump, and they usually don't. However, surface plugs, especially small poppers, can make them act like tarpon when they get fooled in 2 to 3 feet of water. Jigs bounced along the bottom, or jointed swimming plugs working through the middle of the shallow-water column, will catch bass, but not as delightfully as an effectively worked stop-and-pop contest between you and the fish.

The trick is to spot the bass, immediately determine which direction it is heading, then adroitly drop a 2¹/₂- or 3¹/₂-inch popping plug about 10 feet past the fish and about the same distance ahead of where the bass is likely to be when you begin to retrieve the lure. After the lure lands, make one or two short yanks to get the fish's attention, then stop. That's all you need. Don't be disappointed if the bass doesn't immediately rush the idle popper. If its forward movement has stopped, wait a minute or so, and then give it another short, quick yank—just one—and let it sit still.

The next few minutes of inactivity on your part may be the most excruciating you'll ever spend on the flats. But consider it a test of wills between you and the bass. Who will break first? If the fish doesn't move after a minute or two, give two or three short yanks. If the bass doesn't respond, it's either blind or dead. Move on to another fish. But more than likely, it will make a dash for the popper, traveling swiftly over the bottom. As it approaches the lure, it will suddenly turn skyward with so much gusto that it carries the popper—and itself—out of the water and into the air. That's flats fishing at its best.

BLUEFISH (*Pomatomus saltatrix*)

Salt water's most underrated gamefish are bluefish. Bluefish are not really blue but a sea green above the lateral line and a silvery white below it. They are also known as snappers, tailors, choppers, slammers, or gorillas—as their size increases.

Although bluefish can occasionally be found on shallow flats, they are not really flats fish in the same sense that striped bass, weakfish, or bonefish are. Most fish get progressively more antsy as the water gets shallower and they lose the sense of safety they have in the deep. This is particularly true of bluefish, and for this reason, they do not normally cruise the flats. Instead, they patrol the edges of the flats, in somewhat deeper water, but always with an eye on the flats. When they spot a school of bunker or other baitfish meandering on the flats, they dash in, destroy the school, then quickly return to the sanctity of the deep. Or they might lie in wait

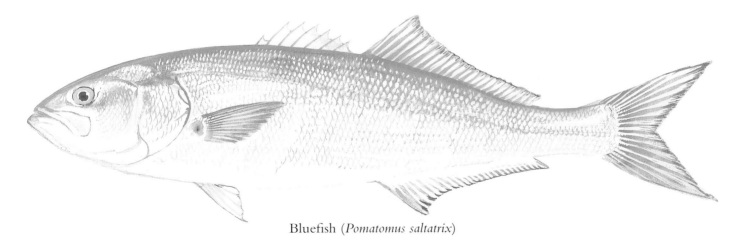

Bluefish (*Pomatomus saltatrix*)

immediately adjacent to the flats, marauding in schools of various sizes, watching for other fish to make the mistake of swimming into their home waters.

Bluefish are so nasty that no other species will join their family: Pomatomidae. Their closest relatives are roosterfish, jack crevalle, and pompano. They are truly a cosmopolitan fish and range worldwide in tropical and temperate waters that do not cool below 60 degrees. In summer along the Atlantic coast, they spread as far north as Nova Scotia and as far south as Argentina. East of the eastern Atlantic, they move into the Mediterranean Sea or even the Black Sea. They are well represented in the Pacific, except for the west coast of North America. Could it be that the Humboldt Current waters, which are generated in the Antarctic, are too cold for bluefish?

There seem to be two bodies of bluefish along the East Coast, and although they occasionally overlap in their range, they do not blend. One group of bluefish summers from Cape Hatteras north to the Gulf of Maine and then migrates south, wintering from Hatteras to northern Florida. The other group summers from Virginia to Georgia, then moves south to winter from Georgia to the Florida Keys and the Gulf of Mexico. DNA testing has shown that they are all the same species, but the cause of the separation has not been determined. Fish in the northern group are generally heavier, ranging from 6 to 12 pounds or larger; those in the southern group range from 3 to 6 pounds. Those that range into the eastern Atlantic are, on average, even larger than those in the northwestern Atlantic.

There is one exception to these migration practices. Schools of very large bluefish—12- to 18-pounders (gorillas)—are often found in the north during the summer, but they do not always head south as winter approaches. They may gang up on the edge of the Gulf Stream, ride it east, and winter off the coast of North Africa. These are truly oceanic fish, and they return to the western Atlantic using the westerly currents just north of the equator.

In late spring, bluefish begin spawning over the continental shelf off the coasts of North Carolina and Virginia. The schools continue spawning as they move steadily northward, following food and temperatures to their liking. They are on the move until late spring or early summer, when they are off Long Island and southern Massachusetts. En route, they produce floating eggs in astronomical numbers. Northwest winds and prevailing currents move the eggs inshore as they begin hatching. The larval and postlarval (juvenile) fish, which are now capable of swimming, feed on zooplankton, enter the bays and estuaries, and disappear into the grasses, where they spend the summer hiding and rapidly growing. By late summer, they reappear in more open waters in the bays in compact, marauding schools of 6- to 8-inch fish called snappers.

Bluefish, like most marine fish, are highly cyclical, with their numbers tending to rise and fall on a 10-year cycle. Bluefish can grow big, and they live up to a dozen years. For some unexplained reason, bluefish grow largest in the eastern Atlantic. Until relatively recently, the largest bluefish ever recorded was a 27-pounder that measured 3 feet, 9 inches and was landed off Nantucket in 1903. In 1997 Roger Kastorsky was fishing on the Five-Fathom Bank off New Jersey and boated a bluefish that was 1 ounce heavier. He thought he had a new world record until it was revealed that a 27 pound, 4 ounce fish had been caught at Graves Light, Massachusetts, in 1982. Digging deeper into the bluefish records, I discovered that the International Game Fish Association's All-Tackle record is a 31 pound, 12 ounce fish boated off Cape Hatteras by James Hussey on January 30, 1972. There is evidence that bluefish up to 40 pounds have been taken off Africa. In the western Atlantic, commercial netters have taken bluefish weighing 30 pounds.

To get so big and fat, bluefish will attack anything they find moving in the water column. They are cannibalistic and do not hesitate to feed on their own kind. They are straight-gutted fish; that is, there are not many rugae (folds) in the stomach lining, which are designed to increase the gut's absorption ability. Lack of these folds indicates a rapid eater. In fact, the food goes through their system so quickly that some of it passes out undigested.

Humans are divided into two groups when it comes to eating bluefish: those that love them and those that don't. The latter generally find the dark, oily meat repugnant. When cooked, the flesh of adult bluefish becomes tallowy because the oils in the lateral line muscle (used by the fish for quick conversion to energy when speed is required) tend to coagulate. Some people will eat bluefish only when they are in the snapper (first-year fish, up to 8 inches) or tailor (second-year fish, up to 2 or 3 pounds) stage. In these young fish, the lateral line muscle has not yet fully developed, and the meat is generally white or light gray.

When it comes to catching bluefish, they are their own worst enemy. They are so voracious that they will strike at almost anything presented to them, and therein lies their downfall; they are too easy to catch. They exhibit the mob instinct of undaunted competition like no other schooling fish. They readily take a fly or plug with the same passion as the real thing. If they miss the strike, they quickly return, because boats and anglers don't intimidate them. Unlike most predator species, bluefish strike their prey's tail. More than likely, they bite off the tail and then return to the handicapped prey, which is then swallowed head first. In most cases, the fly or plug used to catch them need not have a wire leader on the line's terminal end. But when you do get "bitten off," it is usually another bluefish trying to get at the lure in the mouth of the hooked blue. There is an inherent cost in bluefishing without leaders.

Fly-Fishing for Bluefish

Bluefish are formidable on either fly or spinning rods and range from 9-inch young-of-the-year snappers to 18-pound gorillas. A bluefish is never really subdued until it is in the net or flopping inside the boat. Because really big blues seldom make it to the flats and are more

likely to be hanging around the edges, you can get away with lighter fly-fishing gear.

Rods. An 8-weight rod can catch a lot of big bluefish, up to 10 to 12 pounds. Lightweight, graphite rods are a must in 9- or 10-foot lengths and capped with a butt extender. Corrosion-proof materials in the butt end and reel seat should not be affected by salt water. Otherwise, even with a good washing with soap and water, you'll get only one or two seasons' use at best. Fly-rod guides also corrode if they aren't made of the right materials. When buying a rod, make sure that it's really a saltwater fly rod.

Reels. Good reels with good drag systems are critical because of the innate strength of bluefish. The drag control should be easily accessible if it must be increased or decrease while the fight is going on. The initial run, to get off the flats and into deep water, is the motivating force for the first few minutes of a battle. You can let the fish get into the depths if you know there are no obstructions there, but set the drag to make the fish pay for the run. If there are trees, docks, buoys, or anything else that a blue can wrap your line around, you need a rod with enough beef to keep the fish away from them. The reel should be large enough, in either diameter or spool width, to load the backing and line. Even though it is corrosion proof, it should be constructed so that the parts are easily disassembled or removable to be washed.

Lines. A floating line with a short forward taper, and a second reel on a spool loaded with a floating line with a sinking tip, will cover most of the flats scenarios when sight-fishing for bluefish. You need a minimum of 100 yards of 20-pound-test backing line of monofilament, Dacron, or braided line.

Leaders. On the heavy side, leaders in 6- to 8-foot lengths between 12- and 18-pound-test will allow you to conquer most flats bluefish. Because bluefish are not as wary as other species that hunt the flats, they are not especially leader shy. Twenty-pound-test fluorocarbon tippets, 2 to 3 feet long, are sufficient. Add a 15-pound-test snap to the end so that you can quickly replace mauled flies.

Flies. Almost anything that moves attracts bluefish, so it is here that cheap flies might find their niche. Most often, bluefish hit a fly from behind first, usually just inside the mouth and teeth. This means that longer shanked hooks are better designed to catch blues on the first strike. Seldom does a blue totally engulf a fly unless the fly is very small—in which case you might lose the fly as the teeth are snapped shut.

Left: Two bluefish netted at one time.

To attract bluefish, you can work the flies at any depth in the water column, which is usually 1 to 3 feet deep. Start on the bottom with Crazy Charlies and weighted Clousers with up-hooks. Then switch to streamers, such as Deceivers or even Mickey Finns, or bulkier flies the imitate baby bunker, such as the Blados Crease fly. Bluefish are suckers for noisy flies that thrash around on the water's surface, and poppers and even bass bugs are very effective. My only other recommendation is that you bring more than just a few flies to the flats.

Spin-Fishing for Bluefish

Bluefish can be taken on either spinning or fly-fishing equipment, but it is here that the dedicated spin caster has a chance to enter a piscine Valhalla. In deep-water situations, blues first elect to throw the hook and then go deep and act like bulldogs. But on the flats, or along the edges in shallow water, there are only two directions it can go: away or up in the air. Because of this, bluefish have often been called a poor man's tarpon.

Rods. Because bluefish (even small ones) are so savage, a stout spinning rod is your best defense. Pick a 7- to 8-foot rod with a very stiff tip that will take some energy to bend and a comparable butt section, because that is where the fight will center. Pick one made of a graphite composite for strength and lightness. Make sure the guides have ceramic rings, because there will be a lot of seesawing until the fish is brought to gaff (I say gaff because a bluefish will try to eat its way out of the net before you can get to it).

That brings up another point: bluefish teeth. Their mouths are filled with many short, conical teeth planted in strong, bony jaws moved by powerful masseter muscles. When it comes to teeth, bluefish have often been compared with piranha. And more than one novice has been bitten while trying to release a bluefish or retrieve a hook. There are even a few stubby-fingered anglers who have great respect for a live bluefish. If you intend to keep and eat a bluefish, the only safe way to dispatch it is with a lead-filled priest abruptly applied to the head. (A "priest" is a round, $1\frac{1}{2}$- to 2-inch dowel with a hollowed-out core that has been filled with lead. It is used to dispense the fish's last rites, hence its name.)

Reels and lines. No other fish demands such perfection in the design and function of a spinning reel. Smooth drags, large spools that can handle 200 yards of 8- to 12-pound-test braided or monofilament lines, and easy access to drag controls while playing a fish are what bluefish anglers want.

Leaders. On the flats, where bluefish don't school as much as they do in deep water, and where only a dozen or so fish are swimming together, you might be able to get away without a leader. However, if you don't want to lose the lure, you'd better use a leader. I like short, 6-inch, braided wire leaders that test out at 10 to 12 pounds. Hooked bluefish usually strike the lure on the end first, and it is unlikely that the teeth will reach far enough forward to bite the line. However, if another bluefish is attempting to take the "bait" from the hooked fish's mouth, it can bite into the line. The leader usually doesn't affect the action of lure. If the lures you use don't spin and twist the line, there is no need for a snap-swivel attached to the end of the line. You do, however, need a connecting device, so use only the snap—the smallest one you can find, because no bluefish will be capable of breaking it.

Lures. Although almost anything thrown toward a bluefish will work, some lures are more effective than others. My first choice is a $2^{1}/_{2}$- to 3-inch popping plug worked with alternating stops and splashes, a lot like a fly fisher's bass bug. The stop-and-go technique drives bluefish crazy. Second best is a small silver- or gold-colored spoon that wobbles. Here, a slow, steady retrieve works best. For the blue that's looking for food in the flat's substrate, a small, $^{1}/_{4}$-ounce jig of almost any color will work when bounced and dropped intermittently along the sand or mud. Hot new lures, such as a small, weighted plastic shad, are also very effective, but after two or three fish, there isn't much left to attract a bluefish.

Another lure that is very effective is a small (3- to 4-inch) jointed plug designed to swim just under the surface. Pick a mackerel or rainbow trout pattern, remove the first treble hook, and replace the tail treble hook with a single hook. If you don't do this, the bluefish is liable to deep-throat the lure, and you'll have to kill the fish to get the lure and hooks out of its mouth. The only problem with using these lures is that after being attacked by half a dozen blues, there won't be much left.

WEAKFISH (*Cynoscion regalis*)

Weakfish are members of the drum family, and as in all croakers, the males have an air bladder that emits a drumming or croaking sound. There are six species in this genus, but only two are found in Atlantic waters. The species that inhabit the waters from the Bay of Fundy, between New Brunswick and Nova Scotia, southward to Mobile Bay (Alabama) are called weakfish, squeteague, tide runners, sea trout, or gray trout. The greatest concentration of weakfish is far more limited, however, occurring between Cape Cod and Savannah, Georgia. They spawn on shoals in shallow bays from Maine south to the Savannah River, which separates South Carolina and Georgia. Their major spawning grounds, however, are the Peconic bays between Long Island's North and South Forks, Delaware Bay and the Virginia portion of Chesapeake Bay, and south to Currituck Sound off North Carolina.

Weakfish are not the ideal flats species, because their time in shallow water is abbreviated in comparison to striped bass or fluke. In spring, while offshore, they move north in large schools and gradually head inshore looking for water temperatures of 60 degrees or better. The northern portion of this massive school first appears on the flats off Long Island, New York, and other northeastern states around the last week of April, but a week or two earlier in the mid-Atlantic states. Strangely, parts of the school move inshore but don't spawn until later,

This netted weakfish bumped 12 pounds on the scale.

Weakfish (*Cynoscion regalis*)

in summer or even early fall. This later spawning occurs off the flats in deeper water.

During the spring spawning period, the fish don't move immediately onto the flats but gather in deep holes adjacent to these shallow waters. When the time and temperature are right, they move into the shallows. Spawning usually takes place after sunset and continues into the night. Even though the rite is finished by dawn, the fish may linger on the flats for the next day or two. How long they hold there depends on the water temperature: the warmer the water, the shorter the spawning period. When they are on the flats, not all weakfish are in a feeding mood, nor (as noted earlier) are they all in a spawning mood. Those that spawn early remain in the school, and it is these fish that take large, long flies; jelly worms rigged Texas style; and jigs such as the once-popular Salty Dog.

Weakfish are true predator fish, and most of their diet is composed of invertebrates—clams, snails, and especially marine worms. That is why jelly worms make such good lures. However, weakfish have no compunction about feeding on small fish, squid, or crabs.

Once the entire school has spawned, the fish move off the flats and disperse throughout their summer range, which is in close proximity to where they spawned. Their favorite haunts are large beds of eelgrass, where they look for crabs and small fish taking cover. Summer schools are usually smaller and are often grouped by year class, making it difficult to specifically target the fish. After late June, weakfish feed best during the night, when sight-fishing is impossible. They do, however, have a tendency to gather around docks and bridges where bright lights shine in the water, attracting shrimp and other natural baits. Weakfish are extremely sensitive to falling temperatures in early fall, when they move southward to winter offshore. Weakfish populations are cyclical, and their numbers rise and fall on an average 7-year cycle.

There is nothing weak about the weakfish, except perhaps its lightly constructed lower jaw. A hook can easily tear out if the fish is overpowered too quickly on a fishing rod. They are best fought with soft-tipped rods, either fly or spin. Weakfish, like bluefish, are voracious feeders, and when you have one on a rod, there will likely be others close behind trying to steal what the hooked fish has in its mouth. Anglers often keep a hooked fish in the water just to attract others and bring them within casting range. A landing net is a must to bring the fish into the boat.

Fishing for Weakfish
The correct tackle, either spinning or fly, for taking weakfish on the flats is pretty much the same as that used for striped bass. However, the biggest weakfish you are likely to encounter in these shallow waters is in the 11- to 13-pound range, even though weakfish can grow to 18 or 19 pounds. Thus, the tackle used for small and medium striped bass works equally well for weakfish. Fly-fishing tackle has a slight edge over spinning gear, because weakfish spook easily when they detect motion and noise. A rigged jelly worm makes quite a commotion when it lands, but a crab pattern that lands softly on the edge of an eelgrass bed is like feeding them candy. Equally irresistible are full-bodied flies that resemble baby or peanut bunker (Crease flies), especially those with large eyes. Up-flies, such as Clouser's Deep Minnow or even Crazy Charlies, also do well on the flats.

SPOTTED SEA TROUT (*Cynoscion nebulosus*)
Also known as southern weakfish, speckled trout ("specks"), paper mouth, and yellow mouth, spotted sea trout inhabit the waters from the lower Chesapeake Bay south to the Gulf of Mexico and even as far as the Yucatan Peninsula. In the northern part of their range, their distribution overlaps that of the northern weakfish. They are the number-one gamefish in Florida and Louisiana, and probably in Georgia, South Carolina, and Texas as well.

Like their kissing cousins the weakfish, they too are capable of spawning from April to September, although the great majority do so in early spring. The act usually occurs just after sunset, and you can tell when this is about to happen because the males begin drumming or croaking at a ferocious rate. Sea trout prefer their ambient water on the warm side, between 65 and 75 degrees. They may linger on the flats long after striped bass head for cooler, deeper water.

In the fall, spotted sea trout, like bass and weakfish, move offshore and winter in waters 30 to 50 feet deep over the continental shelf, not too far off the coast of Virginia and North Carolina. In contrast, speckled trout found from South Carolina to the Yucatan are less migratory and often live out their entire lives within one estuary-river system, seldom moving more than a dozen miles from where they were hatched. In these more southerly waters, spawning can begin as early as February.

During the colder months of the year, salinity plays an important role in determining where these fish call home. With the chill coming on, fish at the northern edge of their range tend to move farther up an estuary, closer to the freshwater river that feeds it. This phenomenon creates two kinds of anglers who fish for sea trout: those who prefer to fish in winter, and those who like to fish in their shirtsleeves. In reality, summer anglers are targeting bigger fish that are piscivorous.

Like weakfish, sea trout abundance is cyclical in nature, with an average cycle lasting about 10 years. In that period, some fish can grow as big as 16 pounds if there is an abundance of food. However, sea trout larger than 10 pounds are rare. Their favorite foods are shrimp, crabs, and such fish as small bunker (menhaden), Atlantic croaker, spot, anchovies, and silversides. Their favorite haunts are tidal estuaries with soft sand or muddy bottoms. If you have trouble finding sea trout, grab your binoculars and look for feeding gulls. There are sure to be feeding trout beneath them.

Sea trout are not related in any way to real trout. Only their shape and coloration make them appear to be kin to the speckled brook trout. However, they do have one thing in common: smaller foods, such as shrimp and crustaceans, dominate their diets during the first two years (or less than 15 inches), and then they become more carnivorous, switching to foods such as small fish, specifically mullet, croaker, and peanut bunker.

Specks are taken on all kinds of tackle and all kinds of baits, as well as artificials. But fly-fishing or light spinning gear is the only option when sight-fishing on the flats. This equipment can deliver light lures that land almost noiselessly on the water.

Fly-Fishing for Spotted Sea Trout

If you are looking for larger specks, switch to larger flies and baits. Long streamers that imitate bunker and silversides are favorites, and Clousers and Deceivers are also good choices. Don't forget popping bugs, because sea trout love the splash they make on the surface.

Spin-Fishing for Spotted Sea Trout

With spinning gear, 2- and 3-inch poppers seem to work better than bigger plugs. Small gold or silver spoons are also effective, as are soft plastic shad baits or small bucktail jigs that are slowly, methodically bounced along the bottom from a drifting boat. Small joined plugs in mackerel or rainbow trout patterns, all under 3 inches, are devastating on sea trout when worked just under the surface in shallow water.

FLUKE, OR SUMMER FLOUNDER
(*Paralichthys dentatus*)

Few anglers realize the aggressive, predacious nature of the fluke until they see these fish chase their lures in shallow water. They seem bent on self-destruction as they pursue the lure to the side of the boat or even onto the sands of the beach. With their tooth-lined, sinister-looking, left-sided mouths, they rival bluefish in their tenacity and voraciousness. In other words, fluke too are nasty fish, which is their undoing when targeted by sight fishers.

Although fluke are distributed in the Atlantic from Nova Scotia to southern Florida, they are most numerous during the summer months (hence the name summer flounder) between Cape Cod and Cape Hatteras, with the greatest concentrations in Chesapeake Bay. Anglers on Long Island and along the Jersey shore, however, might dispute this statement.

Fluke do not escape the winter's cold water by migrating south; instead, they migrate en masse offshore, looking for the warmer, deeper water along the edge of the continental shelf. They head east from mid-September to December and spawn while under way. Some researchers believe that the fish divide into two distinct stocks—one north and one south of Cape Hatteras—before the outward migration. Others believe that there are four stocks: a New England group, a New York and New Jersey group, the Delaware and Chesapeake bays

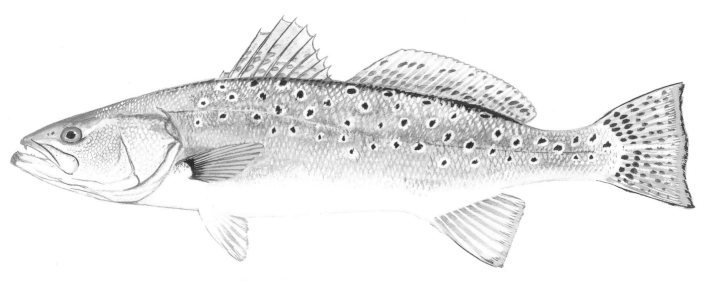

Spotted sea trout (*Cynoscion nebulosus*)

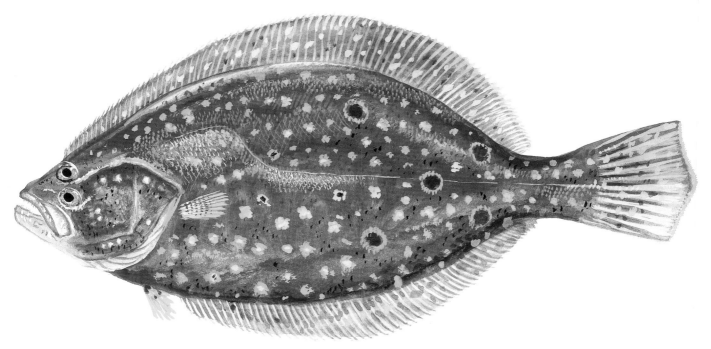

Fluke (summer flounder) (*Paralichthys dentatus*)

group, and one from Virginia southward. Among the stocks south of Cape Hatteras, spawning occurs later and depends on cooling water for the fish to become active. The initial fall migration is along shore as schools combine with others in the vicinity before they all turn seaward.

Migrating fluke have a unique organizational scheme. Rather than moving as a well-rounded, equally distributed school, the fish form two, three, or more parallel lines and follow one another, head to tail, as they move along the beach and then at some point turn offshore. In this pattern, they are often as close as the surf and can be seen from the beach. But don't run for a rod when you see this phenomenon. It is often useless to try to entice them to take a lure, because they don't seem to feed when migration is under way.

Fluke settle in waters 400 to 600 feet deep along the edge of the continental shelf from Baltimore and Norfolk canyons north to Block Canyon. In spring, they reverse their direction, stimulated to move by the hordes of squid that winter in the same area. The fish follow their food shoreward and even into the bays and estuaries, where the squid spawn in deep holes close to land. Squid harvesters working on the shelf can predict the fluke's arrival—immediately behind the squid.

The larvae spawned as the adult fluke move seaward, as well as the postlarval stages, are blown shoreward by winds and driven by currents until they reach the inside bays and estuaries from October to May. Fluke are fast-growing fish in comparison to other flatfish. They are

sexually mature at 2 years, and females grow faster than males. Males seldom live beyond 7 years, but females can live up to 20 years. Fish as large as 26 pounds have been recorded. The largest fluke ever caught was 4 feet long and weighed 30 pounds.

Fluke are available to anglers in the New York bight southward to Chesapeake Bay by the first of April. These are usually the bigger fish, from 10 and 12 pounds, that precede the main body of fish. They are taken in waters of various depths, and anglers chasing striped bass and weakfish on the flats are pleasantly surprised when they find that a 6- or 8-pound fluke has taken their fly or risen to inhale a popping plug in water no more than 2 or 3 feet deep.

Fly-Fishing for Fluke

Although a determined fluke is likely to strike at anything you offer it in shallow water, when fishing deep, they have a distinct predilection for big (2/0), weighted, blue or white Deceivers; deep-running, lead-eyed, chartreuse 2/0 Clouser Minnows; or lead-eyed, pink or yellow 2/0 Clousers. I have a friend who ties Clousers with all white dressings, and these always seem to outfish the blue-white or chartreuse-white color combinations. The white pattern must make the big fluke remember their inshore migration behind schools of white squid. Because even the smallest fluke can put up a strong fight, an 8-weight rod is a good starter. However, if there are bigger fluke around, a safer bet is a 9- or 9–10-weight fly rod.

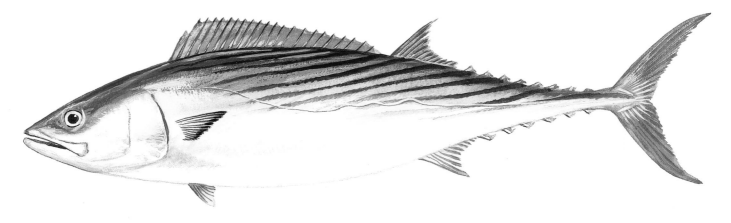

Atlantic bonito (*Sarda sarda*)

Spin-Fishing for Fluke

Much the same advice applies to anglers working the flats with spinning rods. A stiff-tipped rod is in order if you hope to control the action after a fluke strikes. In most cases, a reel with a good, smooth, even drag loaded with 12-pound-test braided or monofilament line will bring most fluke to bay.

Because spinning lures can be noisy and splashy when they land in the water, and especially if the depth is 3 feet or less, small lures are called for. I like small poppers, and it's great to see a fluke rise off the bottom and push the plug into the air as it strikes. Small, jointed plugs also work well, as do small, soft plastic shad baits. The bottom-bouncing baits should be worked slowly but continuously for the best results.

ATLANTIC BONITO (*Sarda sarda*)

The Atlantic bonito, a mackerel-like fish, is sometimes called common bonito, northern bonito, oceanic bonito, belted bonito, or skipjack (not to be confused with skipjack tuna); it is sometimes feminized as bonita. This insatiable blue-water species prefers shallow water and delights in moving inside large bays and estuaries—even in brackish water—or among inshore islands to chase small mackerel, anchovies, bunker, silversides, and even shrimp and squid. Bonito are highly migratory and are seldom found out of schools.

The season for catching bonito gradually changes as the fish move up the Atlantic coast after wintering in Florida waters. In late April, they begin moving inshore at Cape Hatteras. The season is often too short because of the inherently restless nature of bonito. If you find them dallying in one area for more than two or three weeks, consider yourself lucky. By late August and early September, they have reached the inshore waters off the east end of Long Island. From here, some schools move west into Long Island Sound, while others continue northeast into Buzzards Bay.

Like bluefish, bonito feed around the clock, but they seem to feed best, with frenzied abandon, at daybreak and dusk. Because of this seemingly constant hunger, they grow rapidly, topping out at 3 feet long and as much as 27 pounds; they can live as long as 9 to 10 years. However, don't expect to find many of these behemoths. Most bonito you encounter will be in the 6- to 12-pound range. Unlike the almost look-alike albacore, bonito can be eaten and are delicious when smoked.

Because schools of bonito often swim with schools of bluefish and mackerel—probably because they are all working the same pod of baitfish—the key to catching them is to locate flocks of feeding birds. Gulls are the perfect lookouts; don't pay attention to terns, which tend to go crazy over insignificant morsels afloat. Although you can sight-fish for bonito on the top of the water column, the bulk of the school is farther down, often in water 20 to 30 feet deep.

Fly-Fishing for Bonito

Bonito are the perfect fish to catch using light tackle, either a fly rod or a spinning rod. The common factor in both kinds of gear is lots of line or backing, because a hooked bonito can strip 100 yards off the spool before you can adjust the drag. Because most bonito will be less than 10 pounds, a 7- or 8-weight rod will do. However, if there's even the slightest chance of finding a bigger fish, a 9- or 9–10-weight fly rod might be a better choice.

Although you may spot bonito feeding on the surface, don't be fooled into thinking that most of the school is on top. The others are deeper in the water column but will quickly rise to the surface when baitfish are driven there. Therefore, a fast-sinking line is needed; in addition, because of its weight, this type of line can be easier to cast if the wind is blowing. By the time you take up the slack in a cast, the fly is down among the fish. As soon as it begins to move, be ready to set the hook. Actually, just hold on, and the fleeing fish will hook itself.

Avoid using wire leaders just to save the fly. Bonito are known to be extremely leader shy. An 8-foot tapered leader with the last 2 feet consisting of 8- to 10-pound-test fluorocarbon tippet material is standard for a bonito rig. When it comes to the right fly, look for ones with long shanks. Bonito avoid engulfing the fly, but they tend to hit the tail or strike short, a lot like bluefish. The long-shanked hook compensates for this characteristic. Start with Clousers or Deceivers, and pack a few glass minnows on 2/0 hooks.

Spin-Fishing for Bonito

The hottest lure that spin casters are throwing at bonito, as well as false albacore, is the recently rediscovered 50-year-old jig called the Deadly Dick. It comes in five sizes, from 0.3 to 2.7 ounces, and although the bigger ones can be cast great distances, you'll catch more fish using the smallest size. The Deadly Dick comes in three colors: gold, blue, and green. I have found that blue is the hottest color. To compensate for the lighter-weight lures, switch to thinner, braided lines that offer the same test as heavier monofilament lines, but usually at half the diameter. Deadly Dicks are not the only metal that can take bonito. Other old standards include gold or chrome Kastmasters, gold Phoebes, and the Hopkins S-1 Hammered Spoons. Again, choose the smallest sizes.

I have found that for the first week or so when a school of bonito moves into my area, they don't discriminate between flies and hardware. However, they soon wise up to the metal offerings and then prefer flies. You may have to learn both fishing techniques if you want to hurt the bonito in your area.

You can easily handle most bonito on a $6\frac{1}{2}$- to $7\frac{1}{2}$-foot spinning rod with a stiff tip and large ceramic guides. More important is the reel, which should be capable of holding at least 200 yards of line, and especially the reel's drag system. These fish can burn up a poorly designed and poorly functioning drag. In this case, a better, more expensive reel will pay off in fish dividends in the long run.

FALSE ALBACORE (*Euthynnuus alleratus*)

Like Atlantic bonito, false albacore are not really albacore or even tuna; they are members of the 23-species mackerel clan. They are also known as little tunny, Fat Alberts, or just plain albies. These fish are considered both a subtropical and a tropical species, although they do ride the Gulf Stream into southern New England looking for water 60 degrees or warmer in which to spawn. Spawning takes place in June at the northern end of their spring migration, and, like Atlantic bonito, their young of the year have been found in September in Orient Harbor, a shallow bay off the east end of Long Island's North Fork. By that time, they are 5 to 6 inches long.

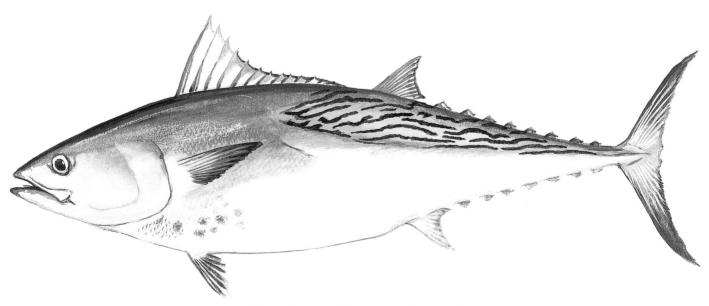

False albacore (*Euthynnuus alleteratus*)

Based on this information, we can assume that we get only one shot at false albacore while they are migrating south, unlike other coastal migrants that head northbound in the spring. Thus, fishing season for adult albies begins in late June in Maritime Canada and Maine waters and gradually moves south as these waters cool with the approach of fall. In early July, they show up in the waters and islands off Cape Cod. By late July, they have moved south and west of Monomoy Point (Cape Cod's heel) and are found on both the north and south sides of Nantucket and Martha's Vineyard. By August, they are off Rhode Island, and in September, the fish appear off Montauk and Orient points on eastern Long Island. The most precocious fish in the migrating schools begin showing up along the northern edges of the New Jersey coast. They may linger in these waters until late October unless prodded to move by hurricanes or nor'easters.

False albacore seem to take up almost permanent residence inside North Carolina's Cape Lookout, in the bays and tidal rivers surrounding Harkers Island. This area has become known for the big albies it produces—often approaching 20 pounds. It is also the area where Pennsylvanian Bob Clouser is alleged to have stopped and invented the Clouser Minnow just to seduce the albies there. They are the same species as the young-of-the-year fish found off Orient Point in June. It must be the food they find en route, over the six-month-long swim, that provides the young fish such a healthy diet and allows them to grow so large.

Although a lot of northern albie anglers may stop at Harkers Island to get their fill of fall fishing, the false albacore don't. By mid-December, the fish begin to feel winter nipping at their tails as water temperatures drop below 60 degrees. They head farther south to Florida and seem to bunch up along a continuous reef 1 to 6 miles off the mainland running between Stuart and Miami. Here, false albacore act differently from those in the Atlantic. According to Scott Hamilton—a skinny-water guide out of West Palm Beach—there are some albies in this area year-round. "The big false albies arrive off Palm Beach in late March. Their numbers increase, building into a crescendo in early May. Large schools will remain in this area through July into late August. This gives us a four-month season," claims Hamilton.

For years, false albacore were considered a trash fish and were merely tolerated by southern anglers trolling for king and Spanish mackerel. They were often frustrated by this inedible fish when schools of them chased their lines and destroyed their baits. Only recently (less than a decade ago) have a few fly fishermen discovered what a challenging gamefish false albacore can

be on the willowy rod. Since then, their popularity has burgeoned.

Although this is not sight fishing per se, except when the fish are blitzing on the surface, albies offer sight fishers a bit of variety. Because these fish prefer more open and somewhat deeper waters, you will quickly become frustrated and discouraged if you try to cruise and search for them as you would on the flats. The best way to hunt for albacore is simply by observing what is happening on the surface around you or by enlisting the aid of birds. With their fantastic eyesight and unfathomable intraflock communication skills, birds will locate albie action long before you will. Follow the birds, and if there are albacore under them, you will see the fish breaking the surface and even becoming airborne, showing off their caudal peduncles and skinny tails. Of course, if all the gulls happen to be at the local dump on a particular day, they won't be any help. In this case, a good pair of quick-focusing, waterproof binoculars may save the day.

In open water, you'll see only the top of an albie or bonito school, which is really somewhat like an iceberg with just the tip protruding from the water. Albies become airborne not because they want to but because, when going after a morsel of food, they rise from the depths of the school toward the surface so fast that the momentum carries them out of the water. If you cast to where you saw one jump, or the ring of the rise it left behind, you won't catch that fish. If you do get a strike, it is probably another fish rising from the depths for your offering. Therefore, deep, blind casting in an area where fish have surfaced may also produce a strike.

A fat Fat Albert.

If the school of albies you are over seems to have moved on, it may be tempting to chase another a school you see breaking water 100 yards away, but in all probability, by the time you get there, they will be gone. The better bet is to wait it out, busying yourself with some blind casting until you tire. Although the fish do move around, popping up here and there, it is more than likely that the albies will eventually return to your initial spot. Another technique that requires a great deal of self-discipline but is practiced by those in the know is to drift in the area where the fish were last seen. Scan the waters around the boat, and note where schools are breaking the surface. This action is often confirmed by a few birds in the air above the melee. Pick one school where the fish seem to be concentrated or are consistently rising, and go there and hang out. Don't be surprised if they actually appear around your boat.

Schooled false albacore are extremely noise sensitive and readily spook if you approach them with the motor running. One technique is to get well uptide or upwind of the school, cut the motor well in advance, and let the boat's momentum carry you on a path that will eventually place you over the fish. I have another technique that works better and with more control. I cut the engine well in advance, lower the pair of electric motors I have mounted on the transom of my boat, and silently creep up to a spot where the current or wind will eventually bring the fish to where I am waiting. A different method is to approach the school at right angles and let the angler on the bow platform cast to the fish. This is very effective because, as the current straightens out the line, it lifts the fly upward on the turn, which is when most strikes take place. It is closely akin to fishing for trout using nymph flies in deep water.

Fly-Fishing for False Albacore

With a fly-rod outfit, what you hope to do is quickly put the fly into the midst of the school. This is best done by using a fast-sinking line and a heavy streamer fly such as a 2/0 or 3/0 Clouser or Deceiver or even a large Crease fly. By the time you take up the slack to begin stripping, you might have already hooked a fish. There are two schools of thought as to how fast you should strip. Some prefer a slow, steady stripping of the line, and others believe that you can't strip fast enough to get an albie's attention. From time to time, both produce fish. I prefer the slow strip because the wall-eyed false albacore are shortsighted, and because of the way their eyes are positioned in the skull, they have no real depth perception. In other words, a fast retrieve may cause them to miss the target.

The compleat albie angler should have two fly rods loading and waiting in the line-minder bucket next to the bow's casting platform. One should be an 8-weight rod, and the other a 9–10-weight rod. The first rod should be loaded with a floating or slow-sinking fly line, and the second should have a fast-sinking line with a sinking tip. Of course, both should be weight-forward lines with heavy flies—1/0 or 2/0 Deceivers, Clousers, or Crease flies—on the terminal ends so the flies sink rapidly with the lines. Leaders should be a minimum of 8 feet, with 2 or 3 feet of 10-pound-test fluorocarbon tippets on the 8-weight rod and 15-pound tippets on the 9–10-weight rod. Tie the smallest snaps available to the ends, because even the smallest is rated at 15- or 20-pound-test. Snaps won't spook false albacore and make changing flies quicker and easier.

The lighter rod can easily handle 6- to 8-pound fish on the surface, and the heavier rod is used when searching for fish in the depths. Both reels should have a minimum of 200 yards of Dacron or braided line as backing.

Spin-Fishing for False Albacore

If you are a dedicated spin caster, you can expect to get albies to take your metallic offerings with enthusiasm for the first week or two after they arrive in the area. Then they seem to become wary of spinning lures. One fix is to go smaller, but this doesn't always work. This can be frustrating, especially when you see the fly casters around you setting their hooks on albies. But even fly casters will find increasing resistance to their big offerings as the season wears on, no matter where you are fishing. The cure is to go to smaller and smaller and to use lightly dressed flies. I'm a firm believer that you can't go too small to entice an albie that has seen a parade of flies in the past four to six weeks.

Seven- to 8-foot stiff-tipped spinning rods can easily handle the biggest fish in the school, even one that exceeds 20 pounds. I prefer braided over monofilament lines because, with the same pound strength, the braided line allows you to cast lighter lures farther. The reduced circumference (surface) of the thinner line offers less resistance as it slips through the guides. Although 200 yards of line will do, 300 yards is better if you find a Harkers Island–type albie.

Metal albie lures consist of anything with some flash. For some suggestions, see the bonito section of this chapter. These lures, especially Deadly Dicks, work on both species.

Fighting a False Albacore

Although false albacore initially make long runs, they prefer to dive near the bottom and fight from there.

Sometimes they quit the battle if they don't feel enough pressure from you. However, because all albies should be released—unless you want one as a wall hanger—the battle should be as short as possible. False albacore would rather die than give up the battle, and sometimes they do. It may not be socially correct in some angling circles to horse a fish into the boat, but that is what you must do if you want the albie to live to fight another day. Most experienced albie anglers try to lift the fish out of the water when freeing the hook and then let it plunge head first, from about waist high, into the water. With this technique, the rush of water causes the fish to open its mouth, allowing water and thus oxygen to run over the gills. It's a lot like priming a well pump to get the water running. There's no way of knowing how effective this effort is, but it's as close as you need to get to mouth-to-mouth resuscitation when a fish is involved.

CHAPTER 2

Southeastern Atlantic and Gulf Inshore Species

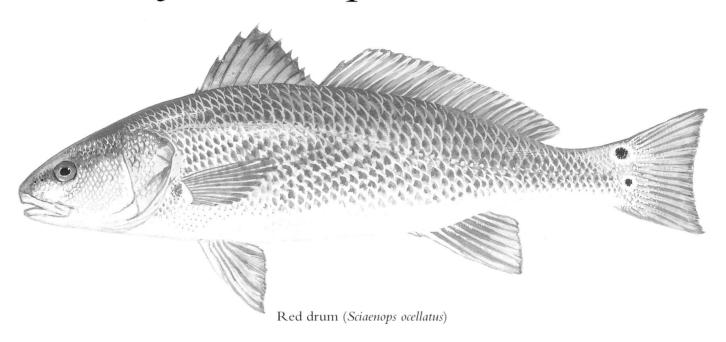

Red drum (*Sciaenops ocellatus*)

RED DRUM (*Sciaenops ocellatus*)

Also known as redfish, channel bass, bull reds (big fish that are usually females and thus cannot be bulls), spottail, or just the reds, this croaker has grown rapidly in popularity among fly, spin, and bait fishers. They are the perfect predator for sight fishers to target because they are found in shallow bays, flats, and tidal rivers. They readily take either a fly or a light spinning lure. As an added incentive, puppy drum (about 30 inches long) make for fantastic eating, which might have led to the species' downfall if not for the efforts of the Coastal Conservation Association (CCA).

The CCA was founded in Texas in 1984 by several wealthy businessmen with a penchant for fishing who set out to save the red drum, which was quickly disappearing from the Texas coast. The cause of the rapid decline of red drum stocks was attributed to one New Orleans man, chef Paul Prudhomme, who had developed the specialty dish "Blackened Redfish." It swept the nation in popularity, and the demand for puppy drum—the

preferred size—skyrocketed. The CCA stepped in and was so effective in its lobbying efforts on the local, state, and national levels that a number of other chapters were spawned along the Gulf of Mexico. Together, they convinced the Gulf states to declare the red drum a gamefish, and as a result, the harvesting of drum was regulated by quotas. Today, red drum numbers have recovered, and the CCA has expanded up the Atlantic seaboard as far as Maine. There are now fifteen state chapters, and the organization has expanded its sphere of concern and influence to include any fish species in danger.

As their name implies, these fish are drummers and are related to black drum, spotted sea trout, weakfish, sea mullet, croaker, and spot. Their range includes inshore bays, estuaries, and tidal rivers from Massachusetts south to the Yucatan Peninsula in Mexico. Large concentrations occur along the Delmarva Peninsula and inside Chesapeake Bay south to South Carolina and Georgia. However, the greatest concentration can be found in the coastal waters of the Mississippi Delta, making Louisiana the best place to be if you want to catch red drum. Unlike most coastal fish, red drum are not transcoastal or seasonal migrants. They do, however, move locally from inshore nursery grounds to deep, nearshore habitats, usually at the mouths of tidal rivers that open directly into the ocean, a sound, or a large bay. Of course, there is an exception to this rule: in northern North Carolina, some bull reds (females) on the Outer Banks move south in fall and north in spring.

The attraction to anglers is strong because young red drum are an inshore species. They don't migrate to join nearshore populations until their fourth year, when they are about 30 inches long. Though called puppy drum at this stage, a 30-inch redfish can weigh as much as 10 pounds, and when hooked, it will fight with stubborn tenacity. From August to November, adult red drum move from nearshore to inshore habitats to spawn. Red drum are long-lived, with some reaching 60 years, although the number of these old-timers has been declining in recent years. In 1984 a giant red drum was taken from the November surf at Avon, on Hatteras Island, that weighed 94 pounds, 4 ounces and set the world's angling record.

Either inshore or nearshore, red drum are easily accessible to anglers in boats, contributing to their popularity. Inshore, redfish can be found in shallow bays, tidal rivers and creeks, brackish waters, and estuaries. You can find them rooting over live or dead oyster beds searching for clam worms (blood- or sandworms). If the water is shallow enough, you can see them "tailing"—that is, with their noses in the bottom and their tails flapping around above the water. When they are on grass beds, a favorite place to feed, tailing is a dead giveaway to their presence.

Not all drum habitat is composed of sand. They also delight in rooting over muddy bottoms, sifting through the silt for clams or worms (similar to bonefish). This activity creates a stream of off-colored water called "muds" by some anglers. The fish are at the head of the trail of muddy water formed by moving currents. When feeding, drum move across a flat like a herd of grazing cows. In shallow water, this moving mass of fish may actually create waves and wakes on the surface. Locals call these "humps"—another dead giveaway of the drum's presence.

Although tailing drum may seem to be in a world of their own, don't assume that their hearing has been turned off. The opposite is true. Your approach to tailing or rooting drum should be cautious, slow, and silent, because they spook easily in these situations. A good rule of thumb when approaching feeding reds is that the skinnier the water, the more wary the fish are likely to be, so proceed accordingly.

Bigger drum, those older than 3 years, spend most of their time outside the shallow bays and estuaries looking for food over more sandy bottoms and in water with a current. The nearshore habitat of the bigger drum is concentrated in slightly deeper water and tidal rips.

Fly-Fishing for Red Drum
At first, fly fishing might seem ill-advised when it comes to a dedicated bottom-feeding fish like the red drum. In addition, you might think that its prominent overbite would make it difficult for the fish to take a minnow-like fly. However, when presented with the challenge, drum can and do rise to the occasion, taking any fly from the bottom to surface. Up-flies (with upturned rather than downturned hooks) make things a bit easier for the fish. Electric or Shrimp Clousers, and even Crazy Charlie patterns, are very effective, but don't pass up a gaudy-colored Deceiver. Crab and shrimp patterns are also effective, because both form a major part of the drum's diet.

Inshore fly fishers can get away using a 7- or 8-weight fly rod. In nearshore waters, a better choice is a 9- or 9–10-weight rod, and a 10-weight is called for if bull reds might be in the offing. Because their preferred inshore water is seldom more than knee-deep, floating lines, perhaps with shooting heads, are a good choice. Nor are drum especially leader shy, and an 8-pound-test tippet works on most inside fish—if it isn't spawning season. At these times, the big drum leave nearshore habitats and work inside waters. And although drum are seldom found feeding on the surface, the attraction of a popping fly on top is often too much to resist.

Spin-Fishing for Red Drum
Although fly-fishing for red drum is gaining in popularity, the majority of anglers who work the shallows are still using spinning outfits. Inshore, a 7-foot, stiff-tipped rod loaded with 10- to 12-pound-test monofilament or braided line is all you need. When fishing nearshore waters, a slightly longer rod and 12- to 15-pound-test lines are called for. Although drag is important in either type of water, drum are not long-distance runners. However, it's a good idea to have at least 200 yards of line on the spool in case a world-record fish likes your lure.

Popping plugs work outside as well as inside. It's also advisable to have an assortment of small, 3- to 4-inch shallow-swimming plugs and plugs that run a bit deeper when used outside. Small spoons, usually in a gold-colored version, also attract feeding drum. They are best worked on a slow, wobbly retrieve. Hot bottom lures, such as the soft plastic shad, now account for almost as many hooked drum as live bait does. They are worked slowly across the bottom in short bursts that make them dive and create mud.

BARRACUDA (*Sphyraena barracuda*)

The great barracuda—the ultimate predator—is easy to catch, slimy to handle, and stinky to release. As a result, many anglers have only scorn for this fish. However, because if its toothy grin, ferocious character, and potentially large size—up to 4 feet and longer—the barracuda has earned some respect. And in shallow water, barracuda are surpassed in acrobatic ability only by tarpon. When a big barracuda has the hook set in it, the fish can jump high and wide.

Barracuda have four close relatives: the Pacific barracuda, the northern and southern sennet, and the guaguanche. Like its freshwater look-alike the northern pike (the barracuda's Latin name, *Sphyraena,* means "pikelike fish," although there's no relationship), the barracuda is a stalker, a predator of the first order. They love to lie in wait for food to come their way, but they will not hesitate to chase it. They are especially fast swimmers, reaching speeds of 35 miles per hour, so very little gets away from them. Another advantage of this speed is that few other predators are able to feed on adult barracuda. They can be big fish—the hook-and-line record is a $5^1/2$-footer that weighed 103 pounds—and they can live up to a dozen years.

Barracuda are truly international fish; although they prefer tropical and subtropical climates, they are found worldwide. In the western Atlantic, they range from the mouth of Chesapeake Bay south to Brazil. However, in late summer, they have been found as far north as Moriches Inlet off Long Island. Although barracuda may be present around offshore wrecks and over reefs in 60 feet or more of water, they prefer to cruise in the shallows, either along outside barrier beaches or in bays, estuaries, and tidal rivers and creeks, and especially along drop-offs with shallow water nearby. On the flats, they feed on anything that moves, especially if it is trying to escape. They are almost exclusively piscivorous, but they probably wouldn't pass up a squid or a muskrat that wandered into their vision. Because barracuda are sight-feeders, they don't dine after dark.

Fly-Fishing for Barracuda

Because barracuda prefer to feed on other fish, they are readily susceptible to big minnowlike flies tied on 2/0 to 4/0 hooks and pulled with a fast retrieve. Because of the long length of these flies, a tandem hook is often needed to compensate for short strikes. Where you cast to a barracuda is also important. If you don't pick the right landing spot, they can be easily spooked. Never cast directly to a barracuda or within a dozen feet of its teeth. The fly should always be retrieved in a direction going away from the predator. Colors and patterns are not that important, but the action is: a fast, steady retrieve is best.

Barracuda can grow large, and in the water, they often look smaller than they really are. A 9-weight rod is a good choice. Floating lines are perfect, but one with a shooting head is better, because you might need to make a long cast. The fish's eyes are near the top of its head, which allows it to spot a boat more easily than one might think, and barracuda are easily spooked if a boat gets too close. A wading angler stands a better chance of approaching a barracuda than does one backcasting high atop the bow platform of a flats boat. Barracuda are not especially leader shy, and 6- to 8-foot lengths are sufficient. However, the terminal end should have a 6- to 12-inch braided wire leader ending with a small snap. Otherwise, the first time the barracuda turns to run with your fly in the corner of its mouth, the line is likely to be cut.

Spin-Fishing for Barracuda

Spinning gear should also be a bit on the hefty side, with 12- to 15-pound-test lines finished with a short leader of braided wire. Here too, where you put the lure is

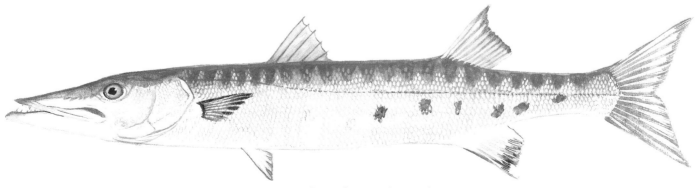

Barracuda (*Sphyraena barracuda*)

important. With its great eyesight, the fish can easily see whatever you toss 15 to 20 feet away from its snout. Small, jointed, subsurface plugs or wobbly spoons, steadily retrieved, are effective lures. Barracuda are not surface feeders, but small popping plugs, worked intermittently, also account for a lot of fish. Sometimes a popped plug left to rest dead on the water for a moment is too much to resist, and a barracuda will charge the motionless popper.

SNOOK (*Centropomus undecimalis*)

Snook is the proto–sight-fishing fish. It is the reason why anglers began wading or pushing boats around on the flats and in the mangrove forests of southern Florida looking for these fish in their favorite haunts. Some anglers might argue that sight fishing began with bonefish on the Bermuda flats or in the Bahamas and that it was the delicious taste of deep-fried snook that caused so many anglers to seek them.

And it was their great taste, especially when served in southern Florida restaurants, that almost did them in. Snook were so strongly exploited in the latter years of the twentieth century, both commercially and recreationally, that they were on the verge of extinction throughout their range—from Virginia (occasionally as far north as Long Island) south to Florida, along the entire Gulf of Mexico and Caribbean coasts, the Bahamas and Windward and Leeward islands, down to Brazil. Even today, this exploitation still takes place commercially. Snook are protected from commercial fishing only in Florida, where they were declared a gamefish in 1957, which prohibited their sale, and in Texas since 1987. To allow better management of fish stocks, seasons, sizes, and slot limits have been imposed on recreational anglers.

Snook are a favorite inshore species and are sought in both brackish and coastal waters, especially along mangrove-dotted shorelines; around bridge abutments, seawalls, and pilings; and on nearshore reefs. However, they are most concentrated in passages, or passes—as most Mississippi and Texas anglers call the channels and straits where back-bay waters flow into the ocean. This fishing takes place during late spring and summer, when snook are moving out to spawn. Here, they aggressively feed on smaller fish, shrimp, and crabs, as long as the ambient water temperature never falls below 60 degrees; at less than 43 degrees, the waters become lethal for snook. This can be a limiting factor in their northern range on the East Coast of the United States. Both Florida and Texas have closed fishing seasons for recreational anglers during the winter to protect spawning fish, so be sure to check the current regulations in each state.

Snook do grow big, and the largest taken on rod and reel was a 53 pound, 10 ounce fish landed in Costa Rica. But snook also have their natural enemies and are relished by larger fish as well as porpoises, ospreys, and herons. The common snook has three close cousins: the swordspine snook, the fat snook, and the tarpon snook. All four occasionally work from brackish into freshwater habitats. The common snook can easily be distinguished from its relatives by its sloping forehead, large mouth, and protruding lower jaw.

Snook are highly prized as sport fish because of their great speed and brutish strength. They can easily make long runs and snap lines in the process. Because snook are also great predators, they like to utilize the water current to bring their food to them. Thus, tides are quite important when searching for snook, with the last two

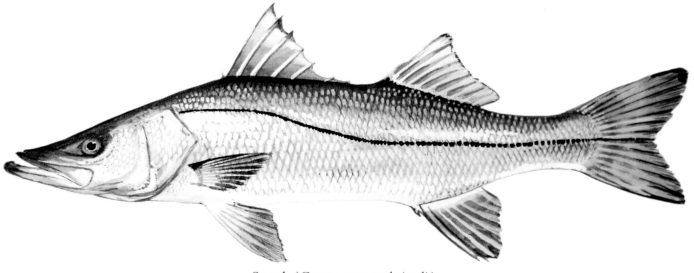

Snook (*Centropomus undecimalis*)

hours of the flood tide and the first two hours of the ebb tide being prime periods.

Fly-Fishing for Snook

Using flies to catch snook is a fairly recent phenomenon. It began in earnest in the early 1970s with Dr. Rex Garrett, who was being poled by a guide on the western edge of the Everglades. He saw what he thought was a big speckled trout tailing in a tidal guzzle. Four casts later, the fish finally took the fly and turned out to be a 30 pound, 4 ounce snook. Because you never really know how big a snook might be, a safe bet is to use a 9–10-weight rod, comparable floating line, 20-pound-test tippet, and a lot of backing on the reel. If you are fishing on the open flats against a mangrove forest, you might even switch to a 10-weight fly rod. This might be the only way you can persuade a snook bent on going into the woods to turn away.

Fishing the flats with clear-water visibility, Deceivers and upturned Clousers might be your first choice, but don't overlook shrimp and crab flies. Small poppers are also very effective.

Spin-Fishing for Snook

Like fly rods, spinning rods for snook should be a bit on the heavy side, even though you might think that light tackle is the way to go. If you are fishing anywhere with mangrove stands, you have to be able to control the direction of the snook. Once inside the "woods," the line can easily be cut by the mangroves.

My first choice for spinning gear is an 8- to 8½-foot rod with a stiff tip and a lot of backbone. Braided line that tests out at 15 or 20 pounds and a large-diameter reel capable of holding 100 to 200 yards of 8- or 10-pound-test monofilament line are required.

Here too, my favorite snook lures are small poppers, 2 to 3 inches long with a single hook. Many poppers come with double trebles, and cutting off the front hook might negatively affect the way the popper swims. If this happens, try cutting the hook at the bend so that it still has some weight. Work the popper slowly, with fairly long pauses between snaps. With a pop-and-stop technique, you'll drive the snook out of its mind and cause it to rush the lure.

JACK CREVALLE (*Caranx hippos*)

Jack crevalle, alias jackfish, are pelagic (deep-water) fish and are not as likely to be found inshore as other sight-fishing species are. And it seems that the older and larger they become, the more solitary they are and the deeper the waters they frequent. Some have been found in water more than 300 feet deep. Both juvenile and adult

Jack crevalle (*Caranx hippos*)

jacks are schooling fish, especially when inshore and in shallower environments.

They are members of the Carangidae family, which also includes pompano, and they are closely related to permit, amberjack, and bluefish. Crevalle are an exclusively western Atlantic fish with an extreme range from Nova Scotia to Uruguay. However, their fishable presence along the coast is much smaller, from North Carolina to Venezuela and among the islands in the eastern Gulf of Mexico and the Caribbean. The greatest concentrations occur along the Texas coast east to western Florida.

Four prominent features—large eyes, a blunt head with a mouth on the bottom of the snout, a deeply forked tail, and no scales on the throat—readily distinguish the jack crevalle from other closely related jacks. In addition, its bluish silver body is offset by flashes of yellow on all its fins. If the fish have been on the flats for a while, the yellow fades in intensity. Most inshore jacks range from 3 to 5 pounds, and this is the size caught by the majority of sight fishers. Female jacks can grow large (surpassing males) and beefy, with some topping 50 pounds and nearly 4 feet in length. From the location of the mouth, it is obvious that these fish do a lot of feeding on the bottom, rooting for mollusks and crabs, but they don't mind occasionally looking up in the water column to chase fish. Nor do they hesitate to feed on the surface as they corral a school of baitfish (a lot like bluefish tactics). Like most predator fish, they are diurnal feeders and need daylight to locate their prey.

Crevalle are more important as a recreational fish than a food fish, even though they are landed for the market year-round in southwestern Florida as well as along the northern coast of the Gulf of Mexico. Look for jacks anywhere you find schooling baitfish: open flats, backwater lagoons, edges of mangrove tangles. When schools of baitfish are missing, something has chased them. Look around any man-made features in shallow water—pilings, docks, stone walls, wooden bulkheads—where shrimp and baitfish might gather. You'll probably find a jack hiding there.

Jacks often feed right up in the suds searching for sand fleas.

Fly-Fishing for Jack Crevalle

When it comes to fly fishing, jacks are very forgiving of the tackle you use. They are unsophisticated and seldom leader shy. Use a 5- to 7-foot tapered leader with a butt end that tests out at around 30 pounds and a 16-pound tippet. When choosing the right fly, don't overthink it; almost anything you throw within the fish's sight will attract it. One reason for this seeming abandonment of caution is that these are schooling fish, and they are very competitive. This is an example of mob instinct at its finest.

The weight of your fly rod should reflect the size of the jacks you are targeting. Although some anglers might start with a 6-weight rod for fish less than 10 pounds, they might find it difficult to persuade the jack to come home. At a minimum, use a 9–10-weight rod, which will allow you to handle any hungry monsters in the school. Once you begin targeting bigger fish in deeper water, a 10-weight rod is required. On the flats, a float-ing line does the trick. In water over 4 feet deep, use a floating line with a sinking tip. If you know a few holes that are 10 feet or deeper, a slow- to fast-sinking line works best for scouring the depths.

Spin-Fishing for Jack Crevalle

The jack is a brutish, nasty fish and a stubborn fighter that won't quit the battle until it is boated or beached. Some of the hottest fishing for jacks takes place during the hottest months of the year in Florida: August and September. More so than other shallow-water fish, jacks are easily fooled by a quickly retrieved yellow or white jig, with or without tails, when it is bounced along the bottom. They are also suckers for noisy surface plugs, popping plugs, or swimming plugs pulled erratically under the surface. Action is what attracts jacks.

Spin fishers need a powerful rod to cope with the bulldogging antics of a jack. A stiff, 8-foot rod loaded

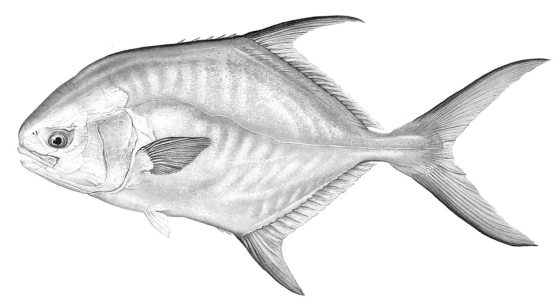

Permit (*Trachinotus falcatus*)

with at least a 20-pound-test line, either monofilament or braided, is the place to start. Top off the end of the line with a strand of 30-pound-test fluorocarbon, then add a snap. Almost any kind of lure will catch jacks. The spinning reel should hold as much as 200 yards of line, because a big jack will run it all out to test you.

PERMIT (*Trachinotus falcatus*)

Permit are closely related to jacks, and at first glance, the two fish can easily be confused, even by experienced anglers. The permit is also known as a round or great pompano, and it has almost the same geographic distribution in the western Atlantic as the jack crevalle. Although permit can be found on the shallow flats around Bermuda, the greatest concentration occurs in the inshore waters of southern Florida.

Unlike jacks, permit are actually shallow-water fish, although they do like to hang around wrecks and structure in water as deep as 30 feet. Permit are the perfect flats fish, which is their primary habitat; they also frequent narrow sandy beaches, the cuts between shoals along a beach, and channels leading from the shoals to deeper holes. There they are fond of rooting on inside grass flats in water as shallow as 2 feet.

The permit's most salient physical features are a deeply forked tail, a blunt nose, and large eyes located almost on the forehead. Compared with the closely related pompano, the permit sports longer, sickle-like dorsal and ventral fins mounted on a silvery, bluish green body. Even though they are delicate looking, especially when small, permit can grow larger than jacks—up to 4 feet long and nearly 80 pounds. The most common size

taken by anglers is about 25 pounds. Permit and pompano of the same size are often confused with each other, but in addition to the longer dorsal fin of the permit, the much larger size of mature adults differentiates them from pompano.

Permit are usually found in small schools of a dozen or so fish, and they feed as a group, scouring grass flats or muddy and sandy bottoms with their low-slung mouths. Permit lack sharp teeth, but their granular teeth form crushing plates that can quickly take care of mollusks or anything else they discover on the bottom. During their first 5 years, they grow quickly, feeding primarily on benthic foods—crabs, barnacles, flatworms, gastropods (snails, slugs, whelks), and sea urchins. Unlike jacks, permit make excellent table fare, and there is a large commercial fishery concentrated in Florida.

The recreational angler's rabid attraction to permit has made it one of the darlings of the flats. The main reason is that these fish are so hard to catch. Many sportfishermen believe that anyone who has taken a permit on a fly has reached the zenith of his or her fishing career. Because these fish are so highly regarded by anglers and guides alike, most are released.

One factor contributing to the difficulty of catching permit is the matter of getting their snouts out of the mud and sand. They feed heavily on shrimp, small fish, and floating crabs, with the last being the permit's Achilles' heel. Although they are taken by anglers in relatively deeper waters using shrimp, live crabs, or even pieces of crabs, more are landed on the flats using light spinning tackle and lures by fly fishers—the preferred method. Two things are required for taking a permit on

Though the permit is the darling of the flats and one of the most sought-after flats species, the fish travels to deep water off the Florida Keys in early May to spawn. These 35-pound permit were landed 4 miles east of Islamorada by Vin Sparano (left) and Captain Al Ristori in 30 feet of water over the wreck of the Eagle.

A quickly subdued permit is more likely to live and strike again.

FISHING FOR PERMIT: TIPS FROM AN EXPERT

Very few anglers have landed more than a handful of permit using a fly. The exception is Del Brown, a California fly fisherman who discovered flats fishing during a visit to Florida in 1974. According to journalist Dan Blanton, for years thereafter, Brown spent an average of 100 days a year on the Florida flats, devoting 60 of those days to pursuing his favorite fish, the permit. An inventive fly tier, he created Del Brown's Permit Crab, alias Del's Merkin. It has since become the most successful fly ever used in taking permit, attested to by Brown's unbelievable tally of 354 fish, three of which were IGFA tippet records.

According to Blanton, Brown believed that five factors combine to make it a perfect day for permit fishing. The first is water temperature—not a specific number, but rather the degree of change from one range to the next. In other words, an approaching cold front might put the fish down. The second is a bright, clear sky that offers maximum visibility in the water. The third is wind. Whereas most sight fishers pray for no wind, Brown thought that a 12- to 15-mile-per-hour wind actually improved flats fishing. He believed that a slightly riled surface in shallow water gives the permit a sense of security. It might also stir up the bottom, exposing many of the permit's favorite foods. The fourth factor, which Brown considered very important, is the tide. According to him, spring tides that create a stronger water flow just after a full or a new moon not only move the water but also elevate the tidal level so that permit can get onto flats that, at normal tides, they would be unable to reach. Brown's fifth and final factor is a guide who knows where the permit are located.

---

the flats: a reel with a generous supply of line, and a means of chasing the fish (by boat) when the end of the line draws near.

Fly-Fishing for Permit

There is no more challenging fish to catch with a fly than permit. Permit are often spooky and difficult to approach, especially in gin-clear flats waters, because they have a well-developed sense of hearing and great eyesight. This demands that the fly fisher be able to make long casts.

Rods. There isn't much of a range when it comes to picking the right fly rod for permit fishing. Most guides agree that a 9-foot, combination 9–10-weight rod is best; alternatively, you could use two rods—a 9-weight and a 10-weight. This will get you through most attacks by permit.

Reels. The reel size is vital because of the fish's powerful—though not especially long—runs before it can be slowed down. Traditionally, these are not straight-away runs but circular ones. Nevertheless, the reel should hold a minimum of 150 yards of 20-pound-test backing, just in case the fish is bigger than you think.

Lines. Lines on the flats are almost always floating lines. If you use a sinking tip in shallow water, the fly won't sink correctly to the bottom. However, floating lines with a sinking tip may be used in deeper water.

Leaders. An 8- to 10-foot tapered leader with a 50-pound-test butt section is what many guides recommend, topped with a 15-pound-test fluorocarbon tippet. Permit have not developed a reputation for being leader shy, but that might be why so many refuse a fly caster's offerings.

Flies. Because of the permit's great penchant for crabs, especially small crabs that inhabit patches of grass on the flats, the crab fly is an extremely effective and popular pattern. For permit, the ideal crab fly is weighted, colored to match the bottom over which it is cast, able to land with only a soft hush, and capable of sinking quickly through the water column. But, unlike other flies used in sight fishing, the crab fly is *not* stripped back to the rod. It must settle naturally into the cover or on the bottom. Del Brown's Permit Crab is an obvious choice, but other patterns work as well, including Jan Isley's Wool Crab.

Spin-Fishing for Permit

Spin casting can be a very capable technique on the flats, even when trying to seduce a spooky permit. The greatest advantage over bait casting is that you can throw a light lure, using light lines, the long distance required to approach a permit from afar. And on a windy day, when fly fishing is nearly impossible, even an intermediate-skilled spin caster can make headway with casts into the teeth of the wind. Even more important is the ability to make quick, repetitive casts to put the lure ahead of a moving permit. No backcasts are needed.

Rods, reels, and lines. The ideal spinning rod is one with a stiff tip, or fast action, between 7 and 8 feet long and equipped with large guides. Most of today's spinning reels have fantastically smooth drags, even the cheap ones. This is important, because when you use spinning gear, most of your battle with a permit is at the reel and at the butt end of the rod. Here, a good drag compensates if you are slow to react to a permit's changing drive. Most reels can be loaded with more line (a minimum of 150 yards) than you'll need to subdue a permit, especially if you use lighter monofilament or, even better, braided lines of 8-, 10-, or 12-pound-test.

Lures. The spin caster's most effective lures for permit are small jigs bounced along the bottom and occasionally allowed to sink into the grass or mud, where the permit will dive for them. And because permit are primarily bottom feeders, the flies of choice are those with weighted or epoxy heads that sink like a lead-headed jig.

POMPANO (*Trachinotus carolinus*)

Also known as cobblerfish, the Carolina or Florida pompano is so similar in body construction to the permit that an ichthyologist may be needed to distinguish 2- or 3-pound specimens of these species. However, on closer inspection, the fish with the slightly longer dorsal fin and a somewhat angular turn in the profile of the abdomen, just ahead of the ventral fin, is the permit. Also, the pompano often (but not always) has a yellowish cast on the ventral portion of the body from the lower jaw to the lower caudal fin, with the color getting stronger along the outer edges. It is no wonder that correctly identifying a pompano can be difficult when you consider that there are twenty species in the genus *Trachinotus*; however, only the permit and the Florida or Carolina pompano are of interest to sight fishers.

A sure sign that the 25-pound fish you just netted is a permit and not a pompano is the fact that pompano seldom grow heavier than 4 or 5 pounds, with the average closer to 2 and 3 pounds; in contrast, permit can range from 25 to 50 pounds. The Florida pompano record is a whopping 50 pound, 8 ounce fish.

Another difference between pompano and permit is their taste. Pompano are considered one of the best-tasting fish of the South, and that was almost their undoing. The gill-net fishery in Florida, which was recently banned, almost eliminated the species, which moves to the Sunshine State to winter. The fish have returned with a vengeance, however. They are found in the shallow waters from Cape Hatteras south to Florida, and they are abundant everywhere along the Gulf of Mexico as well as the islands in the Caribbean.

With the reestablishment of this species in southern waters has come a change in fishing techniques. Before the pompano's return in large numbers, would-be anglers sought the fish along seawalls, bulkheads, bridge pilings, and rock jetties, where the fish found both protection and food. With the burgeoning pompano population in the last decade, the search for this fish has shifted to the flats. The best pompano flats are those with alternating beds of grasses and open sand. These grass flats are where most pompano are now hunted and landed.

Another change caused by the species' newfound abundance is that the fish tend to school for mutual protection. Most fish on the flats now range from 2 to 3 pounds, with a few being a pound or two heavier. This schooling tendency is indicative of juvenile fish and may be the characteristics of a year class—that is, all the fish in the pod are the same age. Bigger pompano are still found in the deeper passes, channels, cuts, and holes and often a bit farther from shore. Water that is too cold or too hot causes the smaller fish to temporarily move off the flats and into the holes with the bigger fish.

Pompano spawn offshore from late March to September. During the remainder of the year, they are inside and on the flats. From time to time, while in the shallows, they disappear. Because of their great sensitivity to cold water, unexpected cold fronts and rapidly falling temperatures may catch them in shallow water that cools too quickly, killing them off. Seasonal declines in water temperature drive the fish south from Cape Hatteras to winter in Florida waters and in the Gulf of Mexico.

There are also local movements of schools of pompano during the summer months, but these are short-lived shifts caused by the tide. Pompano are fond of following the edge of a rising tide as it flows over once dry sand or beds of eelgrass. Here, they are super grubbers and plow though the bottom, searching for sand fleas. Not wanting to get caught with no water over their backs, they move out with the tide. In areas where the flats go dry for a few hours, they wait in the cuts and channels for the water to return.

Pompano have small, toothless mouths located at the bottom of a blunt snout. This is a good indication of where they feed and what they feed on: shrimp; small crabs, fish, and clams; and sand fleas. Foremost among these natural foods are sand or beach fleas and fleas located in the surf, which is the pompano's favorite dining table.

Fishing for Pompano

Fishing techniques and tackle—either fly or spin—for pompano are similar to those for permit. The only modification is that because pompano don't grow as large as permit, you can get away with lighter tackle. Although these fish can grow to 6 or 7 pounds, the majority of pompano found on the flats are younger fish, averaging about 3 pounds. Still, they are formidable adversaries on light tackle, either fly or spin.

Although pompano do fall prey to crab flies tossed by fly fishers, the most effective artificial lure is a small, quarter-ounce lead jig head with a soft, grublike body colored yellow, red, or olive drab. Of course, the jig is most effectively fished on a spinning rod. The jig should be kept on the bottom or just above it in the water column, because pompano are bottom grubbers. A jig in the grass may attract fish, but because most of the pompano's prey is buried in the sand or just on top of it, open patches of sand are the best places to start. When fished on the bottom, especially in sand, the jig is slowly dragged (from a drifting boat) along the bottom. Each time it is pulled out of the sand, a puff of sand or "mud" is created, which pompano interpret as a sign of burrowing snails, fleas, or crabs on the move. In addition, soft plastic shad jigs are very effective on pompano, and don't forget bucktail jigs, which also work.

All this is easily handled on a 6½- to 7½-foot light spinning rod loaded with 6- to 8-pound-test monofilament or braided lines. Normally, a leader is not required, but because ladyfish like to inhabit the same environments as pompano, an 18- to 24-inch length of 20-pound-test fluorocarbon leader might be a good idea. Pompano in schools in shallow water or on grass-covered flats are less spooky than when just a few isolated fish are hunting by themselves. Even so, a 50-foot cast or better is needed. Never cast directly into a school; always aim ahead of or beyond it. This requires rapid decision making on your part. Once you see a school of fish, you must quickly determine which direction the school is moving and where the forward edge of the school will be located just before you cast.

Let the drag on the spinning reel do the work of tiring a hooked fish. Pompano runs aren't long but they are strong, especially when the fish turns sideways and you swear you are fighting a pie dish.

Pompano (*Trachinotus carolinus*)

CHAPTER 3

Tarpon, Ladyfish, Bonefish, and Dolphin

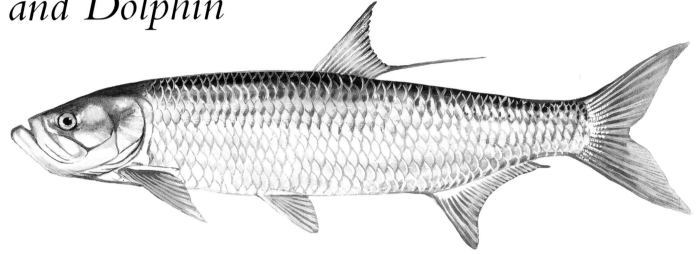

Tarpon (*Megalops atlanticus*)

These three fish are grouped together based on their genetic relationship rather than on their geographic distribution, which is vast and varied. All three—tarpon, ladyfish, and bonefish—are primitive fish, as evidenced by their skull structure, fin placement, and large scales. They are long and slinky, almost serpent-like. Their body structure has changed little over the last 100 million years because their physiology has allowed them to adapt to changing environments. These three closely related species have been termed the "inshore grand slam" by sportfishermen (although some don't consider the ladyfish enough of a challenge and substitute permit in their definition of an inshore grand slam).

This order of fish—the Elopiformes—might be called the leapers, because that is what they do best when hooked on the flats. However, their Latin name actually means "serpent shape." The Elopidae family includes the machete, which is a Pacific tarpon-like fish, and the ladyfish; the tarpon proper is a member of the Megalopidae Family. The latter two are Atlantic fish, and all three can be found in fresh (brackish) as well as salt water. The bonefish is a member of the Albulidae family.

TARPON (*Megalops atlanticus*)

Two species of tarpon exist: the Atlantic tarpon, which swims in the eastern and western Atlantic, and the oxeye tarpon, found in the Pacific and Indian oceans. Although both species are tropical and subtropical in their distribution, the western Atlantic tarpon has been found as far north as the mouth of the St. Lawrence River and as far south as Argentina. Off the continent, in the Atlantic, it occurs around Bermuda as well as among the Caribbean islands.

Along the coast in the western Atlantic, tarpon prefer the warm, shallow waters from Cape Hatteras south to Georgia and Florida; in the Gulf of Mexico, they spread west across Alabama, Mississippi, Louisiana, Texas, and Mexico and along the coast of Central America. They are also found in the West Indies and along the Atlantic coast of South America to Rio de la Plata outside Buenos Aires, Argentina. There is even a contingent of Atlantic tarpon that took advantage of the Panama Canal and found their way into the Pacific Ocean, establishing a colony around Panama's Coiba Island prison. The prisoners are all gone now, but the shallows around the island have produced some giant tarpon.

The two species of tarpon look alike, although Atlantic tarpon females can grow much larger, exceeding 200 pounds. Most Floridians are satisfied with catching a 40- to 50-pound fish, but the Florida record is a 243-pounder. The Texas record is a 262-pounder, and the world record is a 286-pounder landed in Venezuela in 1956.

Tarpon are attractive to sight fishers because of their penchant for shallow-water coastal environments, especially those with riverine characteristics and mangrove-lined lagoons. Unlike some shallow-water predators, tarpon are strongly schooling fish that travel and feed in large schools, often breaking above the surface and resembling a herd of cattle on the move. They can also tolerate low-saline, brackish waters and occasionally trek into freshwater rivers. They may even enter freshwater lakes far from the salt. In these situations, their modified air bladder allows them to gulp oxygen directly from the air.

When it comes to tarpon, the eyes have it: *Megalops* means "large-eyed." Tarpon are herring-like in appearance, with large eyes; large, turned-up mouths; deeply forked tails; and slab-sided bodies. Their bodies provide clues as to where and how they feed. From the shape and location of their mouths, you can determine that they are midwater feeders, searching for their fishy prey by looking up. Thus, juvenile tarpon feed on small foods such as copepods, baitfish, mosquito larvae, and shrimp. As they grow larger, they feed predominantly on bigger and bigger fish but retain their taste for shrimp and crabs. In turn, large tarpon are fed upon by genuine predators—coastal bull and hammerhead sharks.

Few Americans think of tarpon as a food source, but people in Panama (Pacific side), the West Indies, and Africa consider it a delicacy. Although there is no great commercial fishery in the tarpon's range, they are sold in markets in these countries. Everywhere else, the interest in tarpon is restricted to sport. The majority of sportfishermen practice catch-and-release, and in the United States, their take is governed by seasons, limits, and licenses. In some states, there is a no-kill policy. (Note that if you're tarpon fishing in Alabama or Florida, you must possess a special permit if you intend to kill your fish and hang it on a wall.) There is, however, some controversy over catch-and-release practices and the survival of such fish.

Any time is a good time to fish for tarpon, but if you must limit your periods afloat, schedule your trips for early morning, late afternoon, or early evening before the sun goes down. Learning how to catch tarpon can be a slow process, which is fine if you're fishing in your home waters. But if you must travel to seek tarpon, you can learn more rapidly by booking a local guide who specializes in this species. Bring your own tackle, but be sure to use your guide's; it is part of the learning experience. Catching big tarpon is really a team effort.

There is a good reason why most anglers who have fought a tarpon, and either won or lost the battle, reverently refer to this fish as the "silver king." No other fish can fight as strongly and employ such varied tactics to escape, regardless of its size. Once hooked, a tarpon will jump half a dozen times. If this doesn't pull the hook free or break the line, it will take off like a rocket and repeat the same jumping antics. If you are lucky enough to bring it back to the boat, it may jump into the craft with you.

Fly-Fishing for Tarpon

Fly-fishing for tarpon requires more than just basic fly-casting ability; you must be able to cast from 50 to 70 feet. In most cases, the person on the pole can push you to within a reachable distance, but tarpon can be spooky and may take off if you get too close. Mastering the double haul can be a great advantage when fly-fishing for tarpon. This fly-casting technique lets you increase or overload the fly line's inertia, imparting more thrust to the rod and line and thus making longer casts.

Rods. There is a direct relationship between the length of the rod and the distance a line can be cast. Physicists call it mechanical advantage. The longer the rod, the better its ability to add a few feet to the cast. Once your casting skills have progressed to the point where you can cast to tarpon 50 pounds or larger, at a minimum, you'll need to invest in a 10-weight rod, fill the large reel with weight-forward floating line, and carry a spare rod and reel—or at least another reel loaded with floating line and a clear sinking tip—to reach tarpon on the edge of the flats. To be fully equipped to do battle with big tarpon, you might want to add an 11-weight rod—loaded with floating line—to your must-have list, and another rod, reel, or spool with floating line and a clear sinking tip. If your tarpon-hunting area is prone to windy days, you might need a 12-weight rod with a sinking tip on the line so you can buck the wind to reach the fish, along with an additional reel to fit the 12-weight loaded with an intermediate line and a sinking tip. Obviously, tarpon fishing isn't cheap! If you can afford only one tarpon rod, pick the 11-weight and appropriate lines.

Reels. In most tarpon battles, you'll find yourself fighting the fish from the reel—a lot like when you're fishing with a level-wind bait-casting reel. Therefore, it is crucial to choose the right reel for the task. Compared with other saltwater reels, tarpon fly reels have a larger diameter, a wider arbor, and thus a wider spool, so they can hold heavier lines. In addition, they are equipped with sophisticated drag systems, thoroughly waterproof, and constructed of space-age metals. Again, all this is expensive, but if big fish are your goal, you'd better not leave the dock without such an outfit.

Backing. To keep the fly line on top, around the external edge or outside perimeter of the spool, you'll need backing material. Using the full diameter of the reel gives you a better mechanical advantage (faster retrieve) when retrieving line to the spool. As the line dwindles on the spool, the advantage automatically shifts from one of speed to one of power. On the spool, but under the fly line, fill the void with a minimum of 100 yards of 20- to 30-pound-test backing line. Ample backing will give you more line to cope with a long-distance fish and more power on your reel when the time is right to reclaim that line.

There is a right and a wrong way to load the backing, fly line, leader, and tippet onto a reel. If you're like most anglers, you guesstimate the amount of backing you need, choosing packaged line amounts of 100, 200, or 300 yards. To this you add another 28 to 30 yards of fly line, an 8- to 10-foot tapered leader, and then several feet of tippet. If all this fits the spool, you're lucky. If it's just a bit short, you may tolerate it, but you're not getting all the fly line on the outer edge of the spool, and you lose a degree of control. If you can't get the end of the fly line on the spool without binding or rubbing it against the reel's feet, you'll probably pull all the line out to the backing, again guessing how much to cut off, and then return to loading the spool. Does this sound familiar?

The easiest way to load a spool correctly is have a blank spool of the same dimensions. Start by taping the tippet to the arbor and slowly loading it until the tippet is buried under the leader and part of the line. Then load approximately 100 feet of fly line, attach the backing, and wind the spool until the backing reaches just a bit below the rim. On the other reel (which will wind up on the rod), tie a 3-inch loop on the end of the backing, then fold the loop over the line and slip it onto the spool. If the backing loop slips when you revolve the spool, stop, take off the loop, flip it onto the other side, and take up the slack; it should clinch against the arbor as you begin loading the backing. As you wind with one hand, have the line pass through the fingers of the other hand and apply pressure to the backing, causing it to load tightly, under tension, onto the arbor. Maintain this tension until the fly line arrives. You must also maintain some degree of tension on the fly line, but only lightly, because you don't want to bury the line within the line. When the tapered leader arrives, it should be at the edge of the spool's rim, where it will work best for you. Don't forget to identify the line on the side of the spool.

Lines. The most often used fly line on shallow flats (2–4 feet deep) is a floating saltwater line. A slow-sink line is easier to cast, especially on windy days, because of its thinner diameter. However, a floating line is easier to get off the water and start to cast. In water more than 4 feet deep, some anglers prefer a sinking tip on the end of a floating line; or they add sinking, braided leaders from 18 to 36 inches long to get the fly down deeper.

The size (or weight) of the tarpon lines you choose should be close to the designated rod weight. But, because there is great variability between the weights of different manufacturers' lines, you might try a heavier or even a lighter line to maximize the compatibility of line to rod. Most tarpon lines start at 10-weight and increase to match the size of the fish you're targeting as well as your casting ability.

Leaders. Catching big tarpon demands the best tackle and the best leaders. I recommend that you purchase handmade leaders from makers such as Umpqua or Orvis. Tarpon leaders come in two classes: 16 and 20 pound. Within these classes, you have a choice of 60- and 80-pound shock tips or 80- and 100-pound shock tips, respectively. Start with the lighter leaders until you think you're ready to attack bigger tarpon.

Flies. The number and variety of tarpon flies are almost limitless, and a novice can easily be confused. A sensible rule of thumb (if you don't have a guide looking over your shoulder as you open your fly box) is to match the fly to the color of the water you're in. That is, select bright colors for clear water and dark colors for cloudy, muddy, or stained water. The colors can range from a chartreuse Key Lime tarpon fly to the rust-colored Cockroach patterns, and everything in between. Of course, your fly box should carry both types so you can switch when you move to other waters. Two of the best sources of tarpon flies, as well as leaders, lines, and other sight-fishing accessories, are Burleson Sporting Company (www.burfish.com) and Umpqua Feather Merchants (www.umpqua.com).

Short, fast stripping, with the occasional pause, is the standard technique used by most anglers. Tarpon have extremely bony mouths, so you need sharp hooks and hard yanks—often two or three attempts—to bury the hook in bone. Then get ready for the explosion. When it is over, expect the fish to go deep and act like a bulldog with slow but determined runs. If you do manage to retrieve line, and the fish gets close to the boat, expect the battle to begin anew. The tarpon's "second wind" is actually that: it gulps air, stores it immediately in its air bladder, and uses it to renew the fight. If you forget to bring a net or a gaff, be prepared to kiss your $10 fly good-bye as you snip the tippet's tip.

Spin-Fishing for Tarpon

The great majority of tarpon are taken on conventional fishing gear using bait. However, among the horde of anglers who use heavy tackle and live bait, a few will

PEAK TARPON FISHING IN THE UNITED STATES

Where	When
Virginia: Cobb Bay, New Inlet, Oyster Bay (off Oyster)	July–August
North Carolina: Bald Head Island, Pamlico Sound, Cape Fear River channel, Ocracoke Inlet	June and July
South Carolina: St. Helen, Port Royal Sound	May–July
Georgia: Savannah River	April–July
Florida: the Keys and the Everglades	March (maybe), April–June (definitely), July (sometimes)
Alabama: Mobile Bay estuary	September and October
Mississippi: West and East Pearl rivers, Bay St. Louis, Biloxi and Pascagoula rivers	September–mid-November
Louisiana: Birdfoot Delta, Northeast and Southeast Pass Mud Lumps	End of September–October
Texas: Sabine River; Galveston, Matagorda, San Antonio, Aransas, and Corpus Christi bays; Upper and Lower Laguna Madre, South Padre Island (abundance increases from north to south)	June–October; best August and September

eventually begin looking for greater challenges and make the natural move to spinning tackle.

Rods. The size of your spinning gear depends on the size of the fish you hope to land. The bigger the fish you hunt, the heavier your tackle should be—up to a point. Most anglers hoping to catch immature tarpon begin with a 7½- or 8-foot rod, either fiberglass or graphite. The rod should have a stiff action throughout its entire length, but especially in the lower section, where most of the fighting and bending take place.

Reels. The reel's first requirement is to possess a smooth drag that can be adjusted while battling a tarpon without getting your fingers wrapped in the line. Because of the distances that a large hooked tarpon can run, the diameter of the spool should be able to hold 250 to 300 yards of line.

Lines. At one time, the lines used were almost exclusively Dacron; however, these were quickly replaced by monofilament. Today, these line strengths vary from 30- to 60-pound-test. More recently, braided lines—with increased flexibility—have become popular, and a unique monofilament line composed of fluorocarbon

elements is now available. An example of the latter, called Spiderwire, is 10-pound-test but has a diameter equivalent to that of 2-pound-test monofilament. Smaller diameters mean less resistance and drag as the line spins through the guides. The end result is a much longer cast.

Leaders. The correct shock or leader material is crucial to landing a big tarpon. A 6- to 8-foot length of 60- to 80-pound-test fluorocarbon is a must, especially if there are coral rocks or mangrove trunks nearby. This material can withstand a tremendous amount of abrasion. The type of lure you attach to the line will determine whether a snap-swivel or just a snap is required. Because the quality of the leaders is so crucial, many dedicated tarpon anglers don't bother to tie their own; they opt for commercially made leaders.

Lures. Where the tarpon are looking for food in the water column determines what type of lures you use. Foremost are swimming plugs that travel just under the surface. A close second are top-surface or floating plugs, either swimmers or poppers. Color is not as important as you might think. Tarpon view the plug from below, and

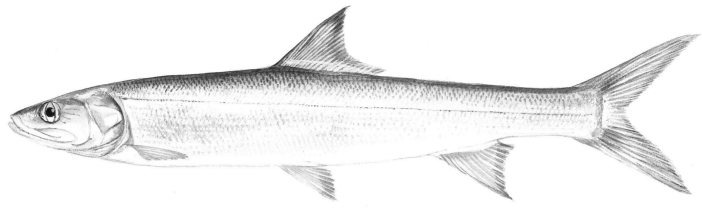

Ladyfish (*Elops saurus*)

everything on the water's surface appears dark or black when silhouetted against the sky. Color tends to attract the angler more than it does the fish. For the latter, the prime attraction feature is the lure's action and how well it mimics the real thing.

LADYFISH (*Elops saurus*)

Often called the poor man's tarpon, this Atlantic light-weight ranges from Woods Hole, Massachusetts, south to the coast of Brazil, although most are taken inshore between Cape Hatteras and the Florida Keys. Few dedicated sight fishers make a real effort to seek out ladyfish, because they are largely only 2- to 3-pound versions of their cousin the tarpon. The Florida record is a "whopping" 4-pound, 10-ounce fish. Once hooked, ladyfish spend most of the time battling in the air. And because they are easily hooked, ladyfish are a great species to use when introducing young anglers to fly fishing.

The ladyfish is a long, slim fish that closely resembles small tarpon. In the fall, they run offshore to spawn, but during the rest of the year, ladyfish are strictly an inshore species. They love tidal pools, estuaries, backwaters, and canals and may even enter freshwater portions of tidal streams. In these habitats they feed on small fish and a variety of crabs and shrimp. When there is a plethora of food available, they school in large numbers and go on feeding frenzies that may resemble a bluefish blitz. Like bluefish, they are voracious feeders. However, most of the time they either are solitary or travel in gangs consisting of just a few members.

Most fly rodders don't make a special effort to entice ladyfish, because they will hit almost anything offered to them. Deceivers are often the best choice when worked off a 5- or 6-weight rod and floating lines. Spin casters load their ultralight rods with reels holding 4- to 6-pound-test lines and toss the smallest spoons they can find. Small popping plugs are also a good choice, but you should replace any treble hooks with single hooks, because the ladyfish's slippery, slimy coating makes it difficult to hold. An even better choice is a barbless hook, because there is no food value in even a deep-fried ladyfish.

Don't put your rod away just because the sun has set. Ladyfish have discovered that the electric lights on docks, bulkheads, and bridges attract a lot of shrimp. The best lure here is a popping plug or bass bug fly. The commotion created by the popper brings the ladyfish out of the shadows and into the light and, quite often, onto the hook.

BONEFISH (*Albula vulpes*)

Tarpon may be the most dramatic fish to catch on the flats; jack crevalle, pound for pound, may be the strongest and most difficult to subdue; and permit may be the most difficult to entice to strike your offering. But the bonefish is the most popular and most sought-after fish on the flats.

One reason for their popularity may be their worldwide distribution, which makes finding them no problem. Thus, mounting a trip to catch bonefish is nowhere near as complicated or as expensive as taking off to catch tarpon, which can be akin to putting together an African safari. Though known as the "gray ghosts of the flats," bonefish are really the white ghosts of the flats. This is supported by their Latin name, *Albula vulpes,* which means "white fox." And they *are* foxy. In addition, no fish makes a more explosive run than a bonefish when it takes a lure and feels the hook.

Bonefish are basically a cosmopolitan, New World fish, restricted to the shallow coastal waters of the Atlantic coast. Along with occasional sightings in New York and Virginia, bonefish are found south to Brazil's most easterly point of land and offshore in Bermuda, the Bahamas, and all the islands of the Caribbean. In the Pacific, they occur from San Francisco Bay south to Peru and west to Hawaii and Christmas Island.

Some taxonomists believe that there are only two true bonefish species, the common bonefish and the shafted bonefish, *Dixonina nemoptera*. Others argue that there isn't sufficient genetic difference between these two to warrant separate species status. More recent DNA studies, however, have shown that there are actually five species of true bonefish. In addition to *Albula vulpes*, there are *Albula glossodonata*, which is the bonefish caught by most Australian sight fishers; the sharpjaw bonefish, *Albula neoguinaica* and *Albula argentena*; and the threadfin bonefish, *Albula nemoptera*. In addition to these five, two others might eventually be considered bonefish: the longfin bonefish, *Pterothrissus belloci*, and the Japanese gissu, *Pterothrissus gissu*. These two are different from other bonefish in that they sport long dorsal fins that run most of the length of the body.

The favorite haunts of bonefish are the shallow waters of intertidal bays and lagoons, among the mangrove forests, up into river mouths, and in deeper waters adjacent to the flats. They feed with the same enthusiasm over open stretches of sand as when they are rooting in grass-covered flats. Like tarpon and ladyfish, they have air sacs or air bladders that can absorb surface air, so when they are in low-oxygenated or brackish waters, they can gulp air with ease. In reality, bonefish and their cousins are primitive fish that have survived the rigorous tests of time.

Bonefish on the extreme edges of their range are affected by cooling waters and migrate toward the equator when necessary. They also move locally, following the flooding tides to feed in newly covered waters and then retreating to deeper water with the ebbing tide. Small fish, juveniles, and postjuveniles are extremely school conscious and often gather on the flats by the hundreds. They feed consistently in an area for several days and then, for no apparent reason, suddenly leave, even if food is still available. However, they don't forget a bountiful larder and will return, sometimes weeks later.

Larger bonefish seem to be more affected by both hot and cold waters. In summer they move into deeper water to avoid the heat and then return to the flats in the fall to feed. Although bonefish spawn throughout the year, their peak season runs from November to June, and they spawn in deeper, offshore waters. No one eats bonefish because they like them—except for sharks and barracuda. And although a few people do eat bonefish and survive, they risk being made ill by ciguatoxin, a poison produced by dinoflagellate plankton that accumulates in the tissues of bonefish and several other species of tropical fish.

Like most shallow-water species, you can learn a lot about where bonefish feed and what they eat by their body structure, especially the head. The bonefish mouth is large and is hinged quite a bit astern of the pointed snout. This is a sure indication that it feeds on the bottom. Like other bottom feeders, the bonefish is a grubber, plowing up the sand looking for worms, snails, clams, or crabs. The trail of discolored water, often called "bonefish muds," is a sure sign that bonefish are in a feeding mood. The mud reveals their location, and if the water is really shallow, about a foot or so, you can also see the fish "tailing"—that is, with their mouths in the sand and their tails out of the water. Bonefish teeth have been modified into grinding plates that are used to reduce clams, mussels, barnacles, sand fleas, and shrimp into palatable, digestible foods.

Bonefish are fast growers, and in the Caribbean and western Atlantic, they max out at 13 to 14 pounds. Those in Florida and Bahamian waters generally don't do as well; some may approach 8 pounds, but most are 4- to 6-pounders. An exception occurs in the back bays of Key Largo, Florida, where a number of 19-pound fish have been taken over the years. Fishing for them is difficult, however, because they arrive in late December and leave by the end of February, when it always seems to be too windy to fish effectively using a fly rod or even to locate the fish in the bay's riled, choppy waters. Bonefish taken from Africa and Hawaii may weigh more than 20 pounds. Bonefish can live in excess of 19 years, and

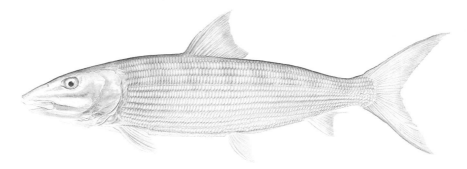

Bonefish (*Albula vulpes*)

either longevity or genetics may be more of a factor than available food in terms of maximum weight.

Fly-Fishing for Bonefish

An angler's gear should be based on the average size of the bonefish in the area being fished. Bonefish sizes vary greatly around the world, and although you shouldn't overdo the power of the rod, it's just as hazardous to underrate the potential size of the fish.

Rods. If you can have only one, choose a 7- or 8-weight rod. If you can afford two, the second should be a 9–10-weight fly rod. If you're fishing the flats around the Hawaiian Islands or off the west coast of Africa, don't leave home with anything lighter than a 10-weight rod. The rod should have a stiff, fast-tapered tip that responds quickly to a change in the rod's direction and doesn't lose energy in the tip's flexing action. Make sure that the guides and reel seat are constructed of material that can withstand saltwater corrosion. Finally, choose a rod with either a fixed or a variable butt extension. The extension serves two purposes: to keep your shirt from tangling in the reel when you're fighting a fish with the reel against your stomach, and to give you greater support and mechanical advantage when it's braced against the back of your forearm.

Reels. The one thing that makes a reel good is a smooth drag that releases without being overpowered to start the spool unwinding. This is where too many bonefish are lost. Reels come in a variety of sizes that are selected based on the weight of the fly line you load on it and the minimum amount and strength of the line backing you put on the reel under the fly line. Bonefish are notorious for long, hard, sustained initial runs. To cope with this, the reel should be capable of holding 150 to 200 yards of backing. Well-aerated spools with plenty of holes in their walls allow you to get down to the backing and effectively wash the salt from the reel after a day on the briny.

Lines. As in almost all sight-fishing situations with a water depth ranging from 1 to 4 feet, the line of choice is a weight-forward floating line. Another floating line with a sinking tip on a spool, a reel, or a complete rod should always be at hand. This way, when a school of marauding bonefish begins to move off the edge of the flat and into slightly deeper water, you'll be prepared.

Picking the correct line for "hot-water" use in the tropics or subtropics is another consideration. Heat has a direct effect on the line's performance, so choose one whose manufacturer touts that it has been designed specifically for warm saltwater use and retains its stiffness in warm-water situations. This is usually achieved when the line is constructed with a braided leader core.

Leaders. Leaders are used when the fly is actually in contact with the fish. If you are not adept at tying knots, buy your leaders at a fly shop or from Burleson (www.burfish.com) or Umpqua (www.umpqua.com). Ten- to 12-foot tapered leaders ranging from 8- to 15-pound class (depending on the size of the fish), finished off with matching 8- to 15-pound-test fluorocarbon tippets, are the terminal tackle elements to use on spooky bonefish in clear, shallow water.

Flies. Patterns for bonefish are often designed to catch the eye of the angler as well as the fish. Just about every fly tier claims to have created the perfect bonefish fly, and they all seem to work at one time or another. What all fly tiers agree on is that, because bonefish are primarily bottom feeders, the hooks must be turned up so that when they're retrieved along the bottom, they won't foul. Most bonefish flies are tied on small hooks, usually size 6, because the fish's mouth isn't especially large. Most bonefish flies are weighted to some degree to get them down to the bottom and make them stay there. Effective colors span the entire spectrum, although pink seems to have a bit of an edge. Some tiers and anglers claim that this is because bonefish are so fond of shrimp, which is funny, because shrimp are actually brownish and don't turn pink until they're cooked.

Some flies are designed to imitate bonefish food: crabs and small fish. Others look like nothing natural found on the bottom, relying on a bonefish's curiosity to entice it to take a look—and, hopefully, a bite.

Spin-Fishing for Bonefish

Spinning gear for bonefish is less complicated than fly-fishing gear because the lure takes the fly to the scene, whereas in fly fishing, the weighted line does that task. This less complex equipment is easier to master, so fishing can be learned more quickly and more effectively.

Rods. As in fly casting, the angler tries to stay as far away from the fish as possible to avoid spooking the gray ghosts. This is done with greater facility and at longer ranges with 8- or 9-foot rods with one- or two-piece construction and medium-action tips. The last feature is required because spinning lures must be light to ensure a quiet entry into the water. Here too, corrosion-proof reel seats and guides are a must.

Reels. Light-tackle spinning reels have reached the ultimate in terms of design and ease of operation. The spools should be large enough, in either width or diameter, to hold 200 yards of 8- or 10-pound-test lines. With spinning reels, drag can be even more important in winning a battle with a bonefish than it is with fly reels, because almost all the fighting is done from the reel and the butt section of the rod. The drag works to tire the fish, and controls for increasing or decreasing the amount of drag should be easily accessible even while the fish is being fought. Easily interchangeable spools are desirable when you want to go lighter or heavier in line strength but don't want to buy a second reel.

Lines. An efficiently working drag system allows you to go down in line strength without fear of losing the fish to a parting line. Monofilament lines have been the standard for the past few decades but have recently been challenged by braided lines. The advantage of a braided line is a 50 percent smaller diameter compared with comparable-strength monofilament. This means that you can throw a lure farther or use a lighter lure and achieve the same distance as when using monofilament. Even more recently, braided lines have been challenged by a new high-tensile-strength monofilament with fluorocarbon materials added. One 6-pound-test FireWire line boasts a diameter equal to a 2-pound-test monofilament. Many of these hybrid lines use fluorocarbons to maintain their strength and reduce their diameter.

Line strength for bonefish battles can range from 8 to 12 pounds. The terminal end of the line should be equipped with a snap or a snap-swivel. Even the smallest snaps test out at 15- to 20-pound-test (depending on the manufacturer), so pick the smallest and don't worry.

Lures. Bonefish feed only marginally on small fish, primarily because most of the time they have their heads buried in the sand or mud. Spinning lures and plugs don't work too well in the mud, but lead-headed jigs do, and they have become the lure of choice among anglers restricted to spinning tackle when sight-fishing for bones. Bonefish, like red drum, permit, and pompano, are true grubbers. Small shad baits made of soft, clear plastic with tails designed to wiggle when pulled through the water, sand, and mud have become real bonefish getters.

DOLPHIN (*Coryphaena hippurus*)

Although Habitat for Humanity has gotten a lot of publicity due to Jimmy Carter's involvement, I had the idea first—except that I build habitats for fish, primarily dolphin. When planning a trip to the canyons off the south shore of Long Island, I take along a week's worth of the *New York Times,* along with a half dozen 2-inch-thick

Dolphin (*Corypaena hippurus*)

sheets of 2-foot-square Styrofoam, the kind builders use to insulate houses. In the center of each sheet, I cut a hole just slightly smaller than the diameter of a 2-foot-long dowel (broom handle), to ensure a tight fit. I then push one end of a dowel into each Styrofoam sheet, and to the top ends, out of the water, I add collapsible radar reflectors. When I'm about a dozen miles short of the canyon I'm going to fish, I stop and begin spreading contiguous sheets of the *New York Times* (the *Times* works better than the New York tabloids, because the broad sheets cover more water). I then set the radar floats in the middle of the newspapers.

I drop these rigs about every mile or two. At the end of the day, when heading back to port, I locate these fish habitats by radar and slowly ease up to them. I can easily see dolphin darting in and out from under the newspapers. When in range, I begin casting flies just short of the edge of the floating paper. There is always at least one dolphin under this new home, and more often, there are a dozen. Of course, I retrieve the Styrofoam and the reflectors for the next trip. The newspapers are biodegradable and disappear after a day or two. This is the ultimate in offshore sight-fishing.

Although many blue-water anglers do take their fly rods far offshore on the continental shelf and even to the canyons, and although they do catch such offshore species as dolphin, bluefin and yellowfin tuna, sailfish, and white and striped marlin, these species (other than dolphin) are not really taken via sight-fishing methods. Most are chummed to the boat, or the skipper happens to cross a school of fish feeding on the surface and may catch a few. However, this is not really sight-fishing and is thus beyond the scope of this book.

FISH MIGRATIONS

All predator fish are migratory, that is, they move en masse from one area to another. Some migrations are measured in thousands of miles and others in only a few miles. Three factors cause fish to migrate: love, food, and temperature. At different times during a season, these factors take turns dominating where and when a fish species will be in a certain locale.

Typically during a year, those northeastern species that winter as far south as Cape Hatteras begin moving north about the end of February. Those southeastern species that winter in southern Florida and Gulf waters begin moving in March and migrate as far north as Cape Hatteras to spend the summer months. These moves are motivated by both temperature and food, as well as the drive to spawn. Predator fish must follow food fish north in order to survive, and these food fish are also driven by the same three factors. The fall move southward is primarily a temperature-related move, as fish seek the heat they prefer.

Not all migratory species follow the same path north or south. For example, when striped bass move north, they take a route as far as 3 to 4 miles off the barrier beaches, yet on their return south, they are almost in the suds. Bluefish usually migrate north anywhere from 5 to 50 miles off the beaches. One reason for this behavior might be that their food (often mackerel) doesn't like shallow water.

When the blues have reached a certain latitude, indicated by water temperature, they make a left turn and head inshore. During the fall migration, the smaller blues head south for Cape Hatteras, but the bigger fish head offshore for the Gulf Stream; some ride it to Europe and then south to northern Africa.

One species, the fluke (alias summer flounder), doesn't make north-south migrations. Instead, in late summer and early fall, they begin gathering along outside beaches and may move along the coast short distances to build the size of their schools and gather all their brethren. Then they head east for the edge of the continental shelf, stopping in water as deep as 600 feet to winter. Fluke begin their shoreward trek in early March. Their primary food during the inshore migration is squid, and they follow their prey into all the bays and estuaries from Delaware Bay north to the Gulf of Maine. (For a fuller description of how fluke migrate, see chapter 1.)

Then there are the blue-water species, the truly oceanic fish that seek warm water throughout the year. They usually grab a ride on the Gulf Stream near the Florida Straits and ride it north along the edge of the continental shelf. They turn shoreward at the various canyons cut 20,000 years ago in the outside edge of the shelf by glacial rivers. These become convenient exits for these fish to head for shallower waters west of the shelf.

Not all striped bass populations are highly migratory. Bass from the Potomac River in Chesapeake Bay are the exception, like this 28-pounder.

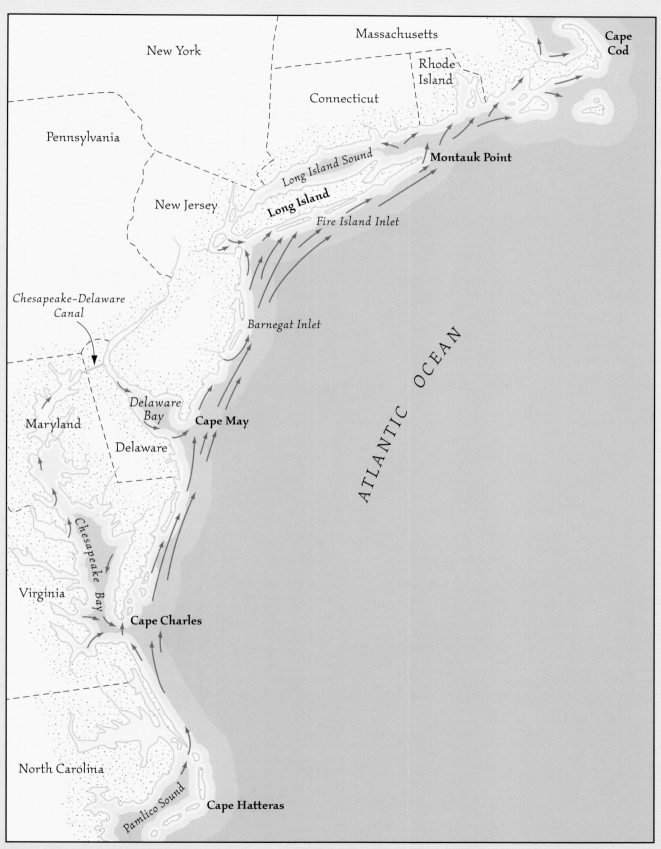

Striped bass spring migration routes. Although not typical of flats fish migration, this illustrates the extreme seasonal movements made by some fish.

PART II

The Tools of the Trade

Now that you possess information about the "enemy," how do you use this knowledge to obtain fishing success? There are several routes to achieving this goal, and the tangible tools required are discussed in the following chapters, but probably the most important factor is your state of mind.

In sight fishing—as in no other fishing situation—your mental state is vital to success. The key element when sight fishing is the ability to concentrate, to focus completely on what you're doing. This is closely akin to a baseball batter keeping his eye on the ball; there isn't much time to ponder between the moment the ball leaves the pitcher's hand and when it arrives at home plate.

In a sight-fishing situation, the need for total concentration is most apparent when you're standing in the bow of a flats boat, searching the water ahead of you for fish movement. The monotony of the scene can lull you into inattention as the boat slowly, continuously moves over clear, 2- to 3-foot-deep water. To spot a fish before it sees you, your gaze must be focused as far ahead of the boat as possible, yet objects under the water's surface must be

Cruising the flats, especially under electric power, gives sight anglers almost unlimited range.

clearly visible. Depending on the water's clarity, a good minimum is 15 to 25 feet ahead. The problem is maintaining that distance, because your sight zone is constantly moving ahead as the boat moves forward.

The natural tendency is to let an object such as a rock, a moving crab, or a clump of grass catch your attention, interfere with your concentration, and stop your sight zone from moving forward across the bottom. When you suddenly realize what has happened, you'll probably find that you're now looking directly under the bow of the boat. And it always seems that just at that moment, your peripheral vision catches sight of a fish darting away, startled by the boat's too close approach. With better concentration, you would have seen that fish in time to alert the person at the controls to slow the boat so that you could make at least one cast to the fish and not overrun it.

Your ability to maximize your concentration on the scene unfolding in front of you can easily be influenced by your physical state. For example, how comfortable are you while standing on the casting platform? The fatigue of standing motionless for too long can interfere with your ability to concentrate. It's also amazing how something as mundane as poorly chosen shoes, a sloppy hat, or ill-fitting trousers can affect your concentration. In addition, your state of mind is influenced by the sun, the wind, the weather, and the temperature, which have a direct impact on your ability to sight-fish effectively and how long you can sustain the effort.

Overall, the better equipped you are—that is, with the right kind of transportation, fishing gear, clothing, and other accessories—the less distracted you'll be, allowing all your concentration to be focused where it needs to be: on the fish.

CHAPTER 4

Boats

Using a boat gives you the mobility to easily and quickly cover vast amounts of water in search of fish. And once you find the fish, you can pursue them. The boat will be your single most expensive investment in sight fishing, costing anywhere from $15,000 to $30,000. The type of boat you buy depends on where you will be doing most of your fishing. You might even be tempted to invest in two different boats to match the waters you want to fish.

There is no such thing as the perfect boat—that is, no one boat will be efficient and effective in all the waters where fish swim. In general, the flats boat is designed to fish effectively in shallow, protected water. The combo boat can fish shallow water to a limited degree, and it can also fish in "light" blue-water conditions, such as along barrier beaches, in sounds and larger bays, and even occasionally out of sight of land. The true blue-water craft can fish from the barrier beaches to the offshore canyons. The price goes up exponentially with the depth of the water you want to fish.

THE FLATS BOAT

As its name implies, the flats boat is a highly specialized craft that is best suited for hunting fish in inshore sounds, bays, and estuaries where the water depth is usually 6 feet or less. Generally, you'll encounter deeper water only when under way to and from the flats. This doesn't mean that you can't fish in blue-water situations with a flats boat, but the weather conditions have to be right to do so safely. The key feature of this boat is its shallow draft, often measured in mere inches. Along with its shallow-water characteristics, the boat's beam is unusually broad in relation to its length. This feature gives the angler in the bow a stable platform from which to cast. These boats are usually designed to carry no more than two anglers and an operator. The boat's hull material can be either fiberglass or aluminum, each of which has its advantages.

Top: The near silence of four-stroke outboard engines makes them popular with many flats fishers.

The main source of power for most flats boats is an outboard engine. Many flats boats are overpowered because their owners have been influenced by freshwater bass boats—the kind used to fish competitively for money and prizes, when time and speed are important considerations. However, in the marine sight-fishing scenario, the engine size and its horsepower should be determined by the weight of the boat and the amount of power needed to push it efficiently. In almost all cases, the outboard is used primarily to get the boat from one fishing area to the next. A secondary propulsion system takes over when the actual fishing begins. Generally, the outboard's size can range from 75 to 150 horsepower, and with the price of fuel an important factor nowadays, it's wise to stay in the lower range. Another choice to consider is the four-stroke versus two-stroke engine. At one time, the four-stroke was considerably heavier than its two-cycle counterpart, but with today's engines, weight is hardly a factor. The four-stroke costs a bit more, but its fuel efficiency and near-silent operation more than make up for it.

Some anglers prefer to have their boats powered by an inboard engine, which is acceptable if you fish waters that are at least 2 feet deep. The inboard is seldom operated on the flats because of the possibility of damaging the screw, shaft, and rudder. Fuel operating costs for an inboard are about the same as for a four-stroke outboard, but the outboard has one advantage: it can be tilted high enough to cross a sandbar or can have a jackplate added to vertically elevate the engine and keep it off the bottom.

The secondary propulsion system for a flats boat is equally important. It can be either a push pole or a pair of transom-mounted electric motors (a single bow-mounted electric motor is not very efficient). The choice between push poles and electric motors depends on where you will be fishing and whether you want to spend the money on motors. Traditionally, flats boats were always pushed by long poles across the flats in Florida, along the Gulf coast, and among many Caribbean islands. Here, the flats are true flats; they have a nearly level, uniform depth throughout their range, with little or no tidal current to combat. In addition, the boats were traditionally small and lightweight.

One major drawback to poling is the wind. Also, the farther north along the Atlantic coast you hunt fish, the greater the tidal currents you have to contend with. North of Cape Hatteras, the greater rise and fall of the tides create currents that can affect the handling of the boat, and in some places, these currents can be extremely difficult for a poler to overcome. Perhaps the biggest downside to poling is that the amount of bottom you can cover is limited by the poler's stamina. In a real sense, poling is strictly for the young and strong.

As flats fishing captured the imagination of coastal anglers and quickly expanded farther and farther north along the Atlantic coast, the conditions under which poling could be efficiently practiced were drastically limited. The number of fish you are liable to spot is directly related to how much flats you can cover. With a pair of electric motors mounted on the boat's transom, the amount of new water you can cruise increases greatly.

THE COMBO BOAT

As its name implies, the combo boat is a compromise craft, designed to operate in two environments. It is not perfectly adapted to the flats, but the trade-off is that it can safely handle the bigger water in open bays, wide tidal rivers, and estuaries, where a flats boat would be in trouble under less than ideal weather conditions. In addition, it can easily handle open-water situations in which land is not too far away.

A poler hard at work.

Retractable, transom-mounted electric motors are the only way to go.

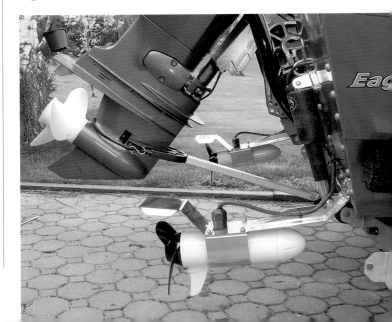

Not all boats are perfect off the flats, but this ChrisCraft Cutlass is as close as you can get.

Heading offshore to look for birds.

The combo boat may feature a deep-V or modified-V hull, is usually constructed of fiberglass, and ranges from 20 to 30 feet long. It can be powered effectively by either an inboard or an outboard engine. It is usually heavier than a flats boat and thus draws more water; however, that is not really a factor. The combo boat can handle four anglers easily, whereas a flats boat is limited to two or possibly three people. Although most of its operation is restricted to inshore and near-inshore waters, when weather permits, the combo boat can make treks farther offshore. If bad weather is spotted, the boat's hull shape allows higher speeds in rough water, allowing you to return to port before the weather turns nasty.

THE BLUE-WATER BOAT

Like the flats boat, the blue-water boat is highly specialized—but at the opposite end of the boating spectrum. Because it is intended to venture into big, blue-water situations, it is a larger craft, usually between 25 and 35 feet, and is often equipped with two large outboard engines. Offshore, it can employ a multitude of fishing techniques, but sight fishing is not one of them.

SHOP WISELY

Before you make a purchase, spend some time looking around boatyards and showrooms. You won't find dedicated sight-fishing boats in every marina or every boat dealer's showroom, but at boating centers along the coast, such boats abound. It's also a good idea to attend a large city's boat show. The one held at the Miami Beach Convention Center, usually in mid-February, is the largest one around.

If you can't make it to a boat show, visit several boat dealers in your area. Compare boat styles, take photographs, and make notes. If possible, take a ride or two on the type of sight-fishing craft you're considering. Even better, find a guide and spend a day fishing on his or her boat. Don't hesitate to ask questions, including what the guide would do differently if given a chance to redo his of her boat. If you like the experience, that might be the class of boat for you.

Once you have a boat, what do you do next? Some boat owners say that a boat is just a hole in the water that you fill with money. That may be true, but it's your boat, your hole in the water, and, of course, your money. How you fill it is your next challenge.

A collection of flats charter boats waiting for their skippers and anglers to arrive at Bud & Mary's Marina on Islamorada in the Florida Keys.

CHAPTER 5

Fly-Fishing Tackle

Fly rods in holders on a combo boat.

Taking fish on a fly rod is the ultimate one-on-one fishing experience. The reason cited by many anglers for not commanding the willowy wand is that they can't learn how to use it, but I don't believe them. At one time I owned a full-line Orvis store and ran a fly-fishing school with four full-time instructors, and we often graduated eighty to ninety anglers a year. I discovered that although there are some people who simply lack the coordination to fly-cast efficiently, they constituted less than 5 percent of the people I schooled.

FLY RODS

In the recent past, most fly rods were constructed of either split bamboo or fiberglass. But bamboo rods were very expensive, and fiberglass fly rods were heavier than they needed to be. The rod-building industry began searching for new materials that were light and inexpensive, experimenting with steel, beryllium, boron, and graphite. Graphite won out, but early graphite rods had inherent problems; for example, the graphite fibers were built to be either stiff or strong, but not both. Years of development eventually conquered such problems, and

modern graphite rods are great performers, lightweight, and reasonably priced.

How many pieces does it take to make the perfect fly rod? Ideally, a fly rod would be made in one piece, but then it would be cumbersome to carry around. If you don't travel in airplanes, a two-piece rod should be your first choice. At one time, three- and four-piece rods were made for packing in your attaché case, but their action was stilted and affected by too many ferrules. Today, with "glass-to-glass" joints, ferrules are obsolete, and the action of three- or four-piece rods is as good as that of two-piece rods, although they are a bit more expensive.

The cost of rods varies greatly and depends on two factors: the size of the rod and the quality of its materials. If you are new to the sport, there isn't much chance of getting a decent fly rod for less than $100. But there is no need for you to drop $800 or $900 for a saltwater fly rod, even if you can afford it—save that money for the reel. Most decent rods designed for use in salt water range from $300 to $600. Other considerations are as follows.

Weight. Rod weights range from 1 to 15. The weight (size) of the rod you select depends on the size of the fish you expect to catch. In most sight-fishing situations, a 9-weight or 9–10-weight rod with a fast (stiff) action tip can handle the majority of fish found on the flats or inshore. If you're thinking about going for tarpon or big jacks, don't consider anything less than a 10-weight rod. Remember that the heavier the rod weight, the more the rod will actually weigh. As a result, big rods are used mostly by advanced fly casters who may work out regularly at a gym.

Length. Usually, the heavier the rod weight, the longer the rod is. For example, a 7- to 9-weight rod ranges from 8½ to 9 feet long. An advantage of longer rods is that longer casts can be made with them. If you elect to use a combination 9–10-weight rod, you should be able to fish effectively in most ranges.

Tip action. Tip action can be described either as fast, medium, or slow or as stiff, medium, or soft. This refers to how fast, in a horizontal test, the tip returns to a straight position after the rod is vibrated. Many rods have the type of tip action printed on the label just ahead of the cork handle. If you don't believe what you read,

Console-mounted fly-rod holders.

you can do your own test: hold the bare rod level to the ground and vibrate it vigorously; then watch how slowly or quickly the tip returns to the normal position once you stop the vibration. A fast tip is needed when throwing heavier flies; otherwise, the loading of the line will be lost in the softer tip.

Rod guides. The number of line guides a rod needs can vary, depending on the length of the rod and how much the manufacturer wants to add to the cost. The purpose of these guides is to equally distribute the line load when the rod is bent. A good 9-foot, 9–10-weight fly rod should have one tip (tip-top) guide, eight snake guides, one ceramic-ring stripping guide (the one closest to the grip), and one hookkeeper guide (usually another snake guide mounted just ahead of the grip).

The rod's most important guide is the stripping guide. It gets the most wear and tear because it gets the first shot at the traveling line, which is often covered with dirt and debris, before it reaches the other guides. Having a ceramic ring inside it guarantees greater longevity for the stripping guide. The tip-top guide also gets its share of wear and tear, and although chrome-plated steel works well, titanium and titanium nitride tip-top guides work better. Some rod makers add a ceramic ring to the second guide, but I think that's designed to catch the fisherman rather than the fish. Some also use ring guides throughout the length of the rod, but this adds unnecessary weight and cost. Simple snake guides are the way to go.

Not every fly rod is made for saltwater use. Unless the guides are made of the right material, they will eventually turn green from saline corrosion, even if you wash them off every time the rod is used in salt water. To make sure the guides are saltwater safe, do a simple magnet test: if the magnet sticks to the guides, they are the wrong material.

Rod grip. The rod grip, or handle, should be constructed of cork, because even when wet, cork will give you a firm grip on the rod. There are several popular handle shapes, none of which has any advantage over the others. Simply choose one that feels good and fits your hand. If you have small hands and can't find a handle that fits comfortably, the cork's diameter can be tailored by gradual sanding.

Most rods come with a full Wells grip. In this design, the middle section of the grip is full; then it tapers both fore and aft, only to flare out again at both ends. The flared foresection of the handle is a convenient place to put your thumb.

Butt extender. Butt extenders are more popular and functional on heavyweight fly rods. The extender is usually wrapped in cork, screws into the back of the rod,

Fly-rod butt handle with a butt extender in place.

and is about 2 inches long. Butt extenders are added to the rod when you think there might be big fish in the offing. In this case, the extender can give your arm a greater mechanical advantage and increased strength by lengthening the handle. It also saves your wrist in prolonged struggles with fishy monsters. In addition, the butt extender keeps the rod away from your belly, a tendency we all share when fighting a big fish. This helps brace the rod and save your arm, thereby keeping the reel and spool from becoming trapped in your clothing.

FLY REELS

The reel's basic purpose is to store the line both when in use and when not, but this is really an oversimplification in sight-fishing scenarios. On the flats, the reel is often used while the fish is being fought. Because the reel is used in a variety of fishing situations, it can vary greatly in both size and construction style. It can be a simple spool on a freewheeling arbor or one that is actually powered to retrieve the spent line. Regardless of style, all reels have basically the same parts.

Saltwater fly reels vary greatly in size.

The reel should be capable of holding at least 100 yards (200 yards is ideal) of 20-pound-test backing of Dacron, braided, or monofilament line, as well as the fly line, tapered leaders, and finally tippet material. Some flats species make great runs and thus require more backing (up to 350 yards) and larger reels, whereas other flats species prefer to stand or dive and fight, necessitating less backing and smaller reels (but still larger than those used in fresh water). Heavier rods (8-weight and heavier) are used with heavier and thicker fly lines to increase the equipment's ability to land larger or heavier fish. When the reel is loaded, the fly line should fill the spool but not crowd the reel seat. Although the reel's diameter establishes the amount of space on the spool for line to be wound, a wider spool is required to accommodate heavier fly lines.

Not all reels are saltwater proof. Make sure that yours is, because no matter how thoroughly you wash it after it's been used, it will never be good enough. Use fresh water and a liquid soap to clean your reels. To aid in cleaning the reel and drying the line while it's still on the spool, many spools are vented on each side with large holes that expose the line to air.

I use a collection of reels that have removable spools that snap and lock onto the reel's arbor. This makes switching line styles or weights quick and easy.

Reel seat. If the rod you're looking at has a sliding ring that pushes over the front and back feet of the reel, don't buy it: it is designed for freshwater fishing. Look for one that has two screw-locking rings. Some reel seats lock the reel forward of the butt end, and others lock it against the back of the handle. In both cases, one foot slides into a deep pocket that firmly holds it there, while the other foot is locked by a movable pocket and then anchored by two large ring screws that lock against it and each other. Reel seats should be made of corrosion-proof materials; the most popular are anodized aluminum, chrome-plated stainless steel, and titanium. Titanium offers both light weight and strength, but it is more expensive.

Reel foot. The reel's foot is the device by which the reel is attached to the rod's reel seat.

Frame. The frame is the reel's skeleton, and the foot is attached directly to it. Frames can be constructed from plastic, stamped metal, or graphite. Better frames are made from machined blocks of aluminum or cast in the same material, which increases the cost.

Spindle. Also known as the shaft, the spindle is located in the middle of the frame and is the axle on which the spool rotates.

Spool. The spool is where the backing and line are wound. The arbor is the central part of the spool—its hub. Many new reels have easily removable spools, a feature that allows you to switch lines and leader weights to match the size of fish you're after.

RIGHT- OR LEFT-HANDED FLY REELS?

The location of the reel handle is a matter of personal choice. However, there is good reason to have it on the right side if you are right-handed and on the left side if you are left-handed. For example, if you are right-handed, you cast with the rod in the right hand. When a fish strikes, the hook is set with a snap of the right hand, while the left hand, grasping the line just before the stripping guide, holds it taut. If the line is played and retrieved by the left hand, the rod still remains in the right hand. You quickly extend the forefinger of the right hand beyond the reel and retrieve with the left hand a small length of line from behind the first guide (the stripping guide). As you do this, you quickly slip the line inside or behind a hook formed by the forefinger, which acts as another line guide. Squeezing the line against the rod with the finger can also act as a brake, or drag. You let line slip out and run over your forefinger only when you feel that the fish is still too powerful to attempt to land it. The fly can be worked with the left hand by grabbing the line just behind the stripping guide and stripping or yanking it in short bursts, releasing it repeatedly, then grasping another length of line to make the fly move and dance in tempting spurts.

However, if the fish is large and demanding and still not in a mood to be brought to the boat, it is often fought directly from the reel, like a big-game or level-wind reel, and not by the left-hand finger. In such a situation, it is a game of give-and-take until the fish is worn down. In reality, a big fish can withstand quite a bit of winding and running off. For a right-handed person to use the left hand to wind the reel would prove too awkward and too tiring. In this case, the rod is switched to the left hand, and the reel is wound with the right hand.

The opposite scenario is true for left-handed anglers. A caveat is in order here: If you decide to switch a reel from right-handed to left-handed, just turning the reel around won't do the trick. You must also strip off all the line and backing down to the spool's arbor and rewind it in the proper direction.

Handle. The handle attached to the outside wall of the spool is used to turn the spool to reclaim line that a fish has taken. One of the earliest features of the first fly reels was a counterbalance placed directly opposite the handle. At first, this was achieved by adding another handle, but they became known as "knuckle busters." Today, unobtrusive counterbalances consist of flat pieces of chrome-plated steel.

Drag. A good drag system is the most important feature of a saltwater fly reel. The drag acts like a brake or restraint but does not stop the spool from turning; it only slows it down. The simplest drag is a click-and-paw system that keeps the line from freewheeling or over-spooling. At best, this offers a fleeing fish minimal resistance. The drag consists of hinged metal fingers that rub up against the cogs of a gear. Experienced anglers can compensate for this lack of a real drag system by palming the outer rim of the spool; however, this takes practice.

Reels with adjustable drag are preferred. Quality saltwater fly reels feature adjustable disk drags that control the amount of pressure put on a running fish to tire it out. The heart of such a drag system is a pad—similar to a brake pad on an automobile—made of material that can withstand abrasion. By simply turning a knob in either direction, you can increase or decrease the pressure the pad exerts on the spinning disk of the reel and thus the amount of energy required by the fish (or you) to pull line off the reel. Setting the correct amount of drag takes a bit of experience, but a good rule of thumb is that the drag should never be greater than the leader's weakest point, either the pound-test or the knots used in it. It is better to set the drag with less resistance and not break the line.

Antireverse device. The antireverse device prevents the spool from rotating clockwise, allowing line to be paid out, unless the drag is set light enough. Such devices are an integral part of reels' fly spool construction; they are also found on bait-casting and spinning reels.

FLY LINES

Unlike in spin casting, where the lure carries the line off the spool, in fly casting, the line carries the nearly weightless fly to an intended destination. Thus, a fly line must have two characteristics: weight and strength. The strength of the fly line is a function of the core material's characteristics; the weight is determined by the coating that surrounds the core. The weight can be enhanced by

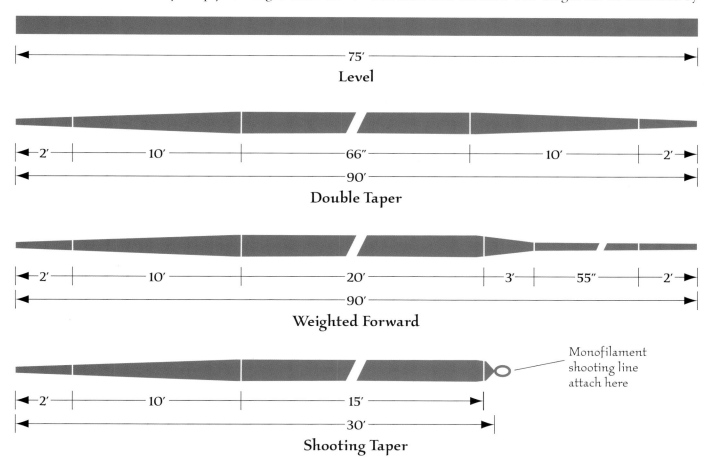

The anatomy of a fly line. ILLUSTRATION COURTESY OF *SCIENTIFIC ANGLERS*

varying the thickness of the coating at strategic portions of the core, which produces fly lines with different shapes. Because, on average, 30 feet of line is extended on a typical cast, the unique characteristics of a line are restricted to that area.

There are four basic types of fly-line construction, but each can be modified to match special fishing situations. There are level (L) lines, double-tapered (DT) lines, weight-forward (WF) lines, and lines with shooting tapers (ST). By adding more diameter, and thus weight, to the forward portion, the line can travel farther onto the water. Lines designated as saltwater tapers and bug tapers are WF lines with short front tapers. This taper allows the angler to more easily "turn over" the end of the tippet when it is tied to large flies, poppers, and bugs.

The density of the line, which controls the rate of sink, is designated by letters. For instance, an F line is a floating line, an I line sinks at an intermediate or slow-sinking rate, an S line sinks faster than an I line, and an F/S is a fast-sinking line. Fast-sinking lines have become highly specialized and are rated (based on their weight) from type 2, a fast-sinking line, to type 6, an extra-fast-sinker. It is unlikely that you would use these lines on the flats because of the shallow-water conditions; however, they can quickly get your fly into the depths under a school of blitzing albacore or bonito.

IDENTIFY YOUR LINES

If you have several fly reels in your collection that are loaded with different lines, you might have trouble remembering which line is on which reel. Using colored line is the simplest method of identifying them. Lines are often available in several colors, but this is to enhance the line's visibility; the color tells you nothing about its characteristics. Therefore, you need to make note of the particular line's weight, taper, density, and any other pertinent information on a small gummed label that can be attached to the reel, directly on the reel itself, or on the removable spool. Be sure to use indelible ink.

Fly reels with pop-out spools.

When the line's construction and density are combined, you get a designation such as WF-6-F: a weight-forward floating line that matches the weight characteristics of a 6-weight rod. On the flats, the most commonly used line is either L-8-F or L-9-F, which is a level, floating line. Because the water is shallow—only 3 to 4 feet deep—there is no need for the fly to get to the bottom, unless you're using a crab pattern. Another common line is a WF-8-F or WF-9-F with a sinking tip. The sink rate can be fast or slow, depending on the water depth and the type of fish. This line is also used in deeper water just off the flats with patterns that imitate fish or shrimp. If there are bonefish, tarpon, striped bass, or jack crevalle on the flats, you'll need longer casts and heavier lines. Longer casts are possible with WF lines but are assured with ST lines.

Another characteristic of fly lines is that they expand and contract in response to the ambient temperature. Lines constructed for cool- or cold-weather fishing are different from those used in the tropics. For instance, a good fly line for striped bass off Cape Cod will stretch too much if it is used in the Bahamas. Check the packaging to see where the manufacturer recommends its use.

On the flats, most anglers can get away with a level, floating line. However, the ideal flats fly line is a weight-forward floating line called a rocket taper (RT) line. This fly line is made with a long front taper that allows it to unfold and let the fly land gently and unobtrusively on the water (not to be confused with the shooting taper, which has little if any line ahead of it). The coating on this line is designed for warm-water use, either in the summer months in the northern ranges or year-round in the tropics. A special coating protects the core from the abrasive salt water. With this line, you can easily make short casts, 20 to 35 feet, or extended casts of 80 feet or more if you know how to double-haul the line. A 9-

weight line weighs about 240 grams, and a 10-weight about 260 grams.

Backing. Not every fish you encounter on the flats is capable of tearing off 100 to 200 yards of line and backing. With this in mind, you can decide not only what size reel you need but also how much backing to add to the spool. As a rule, species such as snook, redfish, bluefish, weakfish, spotted sea trout, ladyfish, and jack crevalle require only 100 to 150 yards of backing line; although these fish are strong, they are not known for especially long initial runs. In contrast, if your game is striped bass, bonefish, permit, or tarpon, you should pick a reel that accommodates 300 yards or more of backing.

Backing material can be monofilament, braided, or Dacron lines. In most cases, 20-pound strength is used because it is bulky enough to put the fly line close to the outside edge of the spool. Fly lines are typically 90 to 100 feet long.

Leaders and tippets. Today, few anglers have the time or the skill to tie their own tapered leaders. It is both easier and safer to buy tapered leaders from a tackle shop or order them from one of the large fly-fishing supply businesses. For most of the action on the flats, you can get away with tapered leaders having a butt strength of 15- to 20-pound-test. For bigger fish, increase the leader strength to 25 or 50 pounds, especially if big tarpon are in your sights.

Leader strength is designated by the X system, with 0X the heaviest and 8X the lightest. I like to take a 25- or 30-pound-test tapered leader and use only 3 feet of the heavier end. To that, I add a 2-foot length of 10- to 12-pount-test fluorocarbon tippet; to the tippet, I add a 2-foot length of the same material in 20-pound-test, which becomes my shock leader. If you plan to make your own shock leader, which isn't difficult, you should

reel line

shock leader

Line-to-shock leader knot.

On a boat, line tenders or line buckets replace the wading basket.

learn how to tie a shock leader knot; this solves the problem of tying a heavy line to a smaller-diameter line. Shock leaders are important if the flats aren't clean or if other predator fish, such as barracuda or bluefish, are watching your show.

To the terminal end, I add the smallest snap available, usually 10- to 15-pound-test. This makes switching flies almost instantaneous. I have never found that the snap deterred fish from striking the fly.

Leader loops. Leader loops have made the lives of fly fishers considerably easier. Some line makers automatically put loops on the distal end of the line to make it easier for you to attach a leader. If not, you can buy these loops, in sizes that match the weight of the line, from tackle shops and stores. Using these loops means that you can avoid knotting up the end of your fly line, which creates bulk and wind resistance at the end of the cast. The loops are attached by a weave, like the Chinese finger puzzle, that tightens the harder the loop is pulled.

Stripping baskets. The purpose of a stripping basket is to store the line as it is retrieved through the stripping guide between casts. Fly fishers use two kinds of stripping baskets, depending on whether they wade or fish from a boat. Waders on the flats wear baskets strapped around the waist; these come in a variety of materials, shapes, and sizes. Some fly casters also wear these baskets when fishing from a boat. The second kind, used by anglers casting from the bow platform of a flats boat, is also used to store the rod when it's not in use. The stripping basket on the boat should be movable, so that it can be located on the angler's right or left side, depending on which one is dominant. The top should be at a level close to the angler's hand at the end of the stripping action, allowing the line to fall into the basket. When stored and waiting for the next cast, the line lies free in the basket and should not be replaced on the spool. In this manner, it is ready to be cast quickly.

In a boat without a stripping basket, the line may be left on the deck, but this is effective only if there are no obstructions in the boat to snag the line. Another technique is to let the line's full casting length, about 30 feet, drag in the water when the boat is moving or lie in the water when the boat is idle. The cast is started with the line in the water, creating drag and thus transferring kinetic energy to dynamic energy in the rod, allowing the cast to be made without making a backcast. This is important when a backcast might spook the fish.

CHAPTER 6

Flies

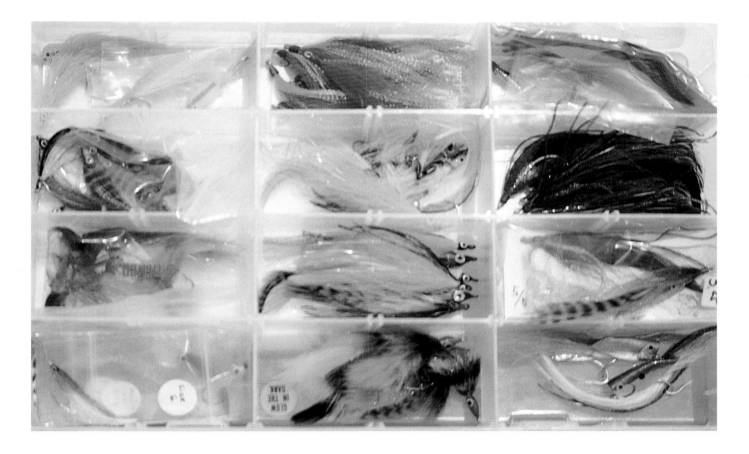

In a saltwater environment, you really don't have to match the hatch to catch fish. Although flies that look like baitfish (streamers) work well, I believe that the fly's color and action are the key features. Hundreds of effective fly patterns are available, but you can get by with half a dozen. The only real variable is the size of the fly. Most are designed to imitate small fish—bay anchovies, silversides, sand eels (sand lances), and bunker fry. Some, like popper flies, don't imitate anything; in this case, it's the fly's action that attracts fish and brings them to the surface. If your fly box is filled with Deceivers, Clousers, Crease flies, Crazy Charlies, and a few Popovic's Bangers, you're ready for sight fishing.

DOWN-FLIES

It seems only natural that the first flies used on the flats were streamers, often copies of freshwater trout flies.

Most noteworthy were the Deceivers, a fly designed by Lefty Kreh but duplicated to some degree by anyone who has tied flies for the flats. These "down-flies"—so called because their hooks hang down or under the fly—also had some inspiration in the 1920s by Joe Brooks and Harold Gibbs. Brooks' Blonde was the rage for years and was no more than yellow-colored bucktails often tied on a short-shanked hook and designed to interest striped bass on the Susquehanna Flats in the northern part of Chesapeake Bay. The Gibbs Striper was a similar fly designed for the same purpose.

Lefty Kreh, originally from Frederick, Maryland, also did his field-testing on Chesapeake Bay, where the goal was to catch striped bass. His variation was to give his streamer a full-bodied look. He accomplished this by

Top: Big fish like big flies, which need a big box.

55

Minnow-like down-flies.

Up-flies scour the bottom for fish.

crowding the hook's shank with extra green and white or blue and white bucktails and adding an eye for fish appeal. Hollow bucktail hairs float, but the additional weight of the hook takes the fly under the surface. These flies are very attractive to bass, which spend most of their time studying the water's surface rather than the sandy bottom.

UP-FLIES

Not all the fish found on the flats swim at or near the top of the water column. In reality, most flats fish are benthos, or bottom feeders or grubbers. That is, they root through the sand and mud looking for food. Early flats anglers who tied their own flies quickly realized that to get down to where the fish were feeding, they needed a weighted fly. So they added a strip of lead foil, as well as eyes, which made the fly look even better. This worked, but a weighted up-fly dragged across the bottom plowed the water almost as easily as a bonefish, creating "mud."

The solution was simple: bend the hook's eye in the opposite direction and secure the floatable bucktails so they came off above the hook's shank. That was an improvement, but there was still a problem. Even though the fly now rode above the sand, it still had a tendency to catch grass and other debris. The answer was a weedless hook, created by adding long, stiff hairs to the fly, starting immediately behind the shank's eye and extending beyond the curve of the hook. Just above the stiff hairs on the shank, more buoyant bucktails were added. Because bucktails are hollow and float, the addition of just a few in the right place on the hook guaranteed that the fly would always swim with the hook up. Thus the perfect up-fly (or inverted-hook fly) evolved.

Although the most popular up-fly is Bob Clouser's Minnow, probably the best known is the Crazy Charlie, invented in the late 1970s by Californian Bob Nauheimal and named after his guide, "Bonefish" Charlie Smith. It was designed initially to imitate glass minnows and attract bonefish on the Bahamian flats. It is a simple fly, lightly dressed with thin body tinsel, tufts of stiff wing hair emanating from near the hook's eye to give it some weedless characteristics, and a pair of large, weighted, hand-painted, bulbous eyes just below the hook's eye. The only variety in the fly is the color, which can be yellow, pink, tan, olive, and gold.

Bendbacks and Keel Flies

Bendbacks and keel flies are slightly modified up-flies that feature a slight downward bend in the shank of the hook just $3/16$ inch behind the hook's eye. This helps the hook ride with the point up and adds to its weedless

character. Instead of a bend, some keel fly patterns use offset hooks that drop the shaft below the eye; the shaft is then bent at a right angle.

Crab Flies

Up-flies can be divided into several groups, and in addition to Clouser's Deep Minnow and the Half-and-Half Clouser, there are crab and shrimp patterns that are excruciatingly accurate in their details. The molded bodies of these flies are formed in epoxy or part epoxy and other materials such as latex and hot glue. When molded in thin strips, latex imitates a crab's legs and adds flutter as the fly is allowed to fall to the bottom. This fluttering action is a sure fish-eye-catcher. Cured hot glue can be molded into intricate shapes that further enhance a fly's attractiveness to a predator fish. Crab patterns are numerous and include such well-known flies as Anderson's McCrab, Del Brown's Merkin or Permit Crab Black and Tans, and Mathew's Turneffe Crab.

One of the most buzzard-looking molded flies is the M.O.E. (Mother of Epoxy) fly. It is an up-fly that sports a triangular body molded around the hook and then adorned with two tail feathers that turn outward in different directions, like spread legs, with tufts of hair around the bend of the hook.

POPPERS

There is little doubt that the first popper-like flies used on the flats were freshwater bass bugs. The transition to salt water was natural and quick, and once the word was out, they became standard in every flats angler's fly box.

Poppers are designed to catch a fish's attention by sound, action, or both. When these surface plugs are pulled on the top, they make a commotion intended to catch the eye of a predator fish. Originally, small poppers were made of cork, with the hook buried in the body so that only the bend and point were exposed. On larger versions, the hook is attached to the eye of the distal end on a buried wire, and the line is attached to the proximal end. Today, most poppers are made of plastics and foam materials rather than cork.

The popper pops because the face of the plug is concave. This allows the popper to scoop up water when it's pulled quickly; the concave surface shoots the water ahead of the lure, creating a splash and often a noise to attract fish. Working a popper correctly is an art, but it isn't difficult to learn. The popper is retrieved not in a constant motion but with a stop-and-go technique in which the stop period is often considerably longer than the go period. Sometimes, a resting pooper is hit by a watching fish, without any further pulling. It's a game of wait-and-see between fish and fisherman.

Noisy poppers create action on the flats.

Examples of effective poppers are Bob Popovic's Banger and Waller's Pearly Popper, and they include a variety of chuggers, pencil poppers, and streakers. Sliders are a variation on the popper theme in which the body is reversed, with the concave or blunt end astern and pulled by the eye in the front. Sliders are used when the sound the popper makes as it's pulled through the water is more important than the splash. Between daybreak and sunrise, and between sunset and darkness, sound is often more effective in attracting fish than is splashing action. In this variation, the hooks are lightly dressed with materials extending well beyond the hook bend.

CREASE FLIES

Captain Joe Blados of Southold, New York, invented the Crease fly in 1982. It was immediately successful because it imitated a major food source for a lot of fish. The fly is not easy to categorize because it can act like a swimming baby bunker in the water or a popper on the water. It might be classed as a hybrid fly—a popper that also works underwater. On the surface, it is fished at a hurried pace with occasional short breaks. Because of its

somewhat cupped face, it creates a tumult in the water that readily gets a fish's attention. If you want to fish it on or just under the surface, it is best worked with a floating line. If you want to fish it deeper in the water column as a popper-type fly, a sinking tip on a floating line works best, or you can use a slow-sink intermediate line. When the Crease fly is fished under the surface, the retrieve is considerably slower, but it never stops.

Sensing that a surface version of his fly was needed, Blados and other innovators began increasing the bulk of the Crease fly, giving it a decidedly stronger punch when popped on the water. In either version of the fly, the attractive, reflective finish and the big eyes quickly catch the attention of fish on the flats or schooling in deeper water. In deeper water, when fished on a sinking line, the fly is likely to be mouthed by any fish watching it descend. The strike usually occurs just as the fly is retrieved off the bottom.

TARPON FLIES

Flies designed to fool tarpon were first developed on the flats in the Florida Keys. The initial tarpon fly looked a bit trashy out of the water and resembled a mess of chicken feathers because that's exactly what it was: a collection of chicken saddle hackle and a thick ring of swept-backed palmered hackle at the hook's bend. The hackle was palmered (attached at the hook bend and then spiraled or wound toward the head, around the body) to create a bigger commotion on the water. Today's popular tarpon flies bear no resemblance to past patterns. They look like needle-nose flies, with long, thin, lightly dressed foresections that, just before the hook's bend, explode in a burst of hairs that look like they could use some hairspray.

The Florida Keys play host to the most famous tarpon fishery in the world, and sight-fishing is the rule. Here, the flats stretch for 106 miles from Key Largo on the mainland to Key West at the tip. Unfortunately, schools of the biggest tarpon show up in the Keys when most snowbirds have already headed north. During the summer months, these fish range from 75 to 160 pounds. Unless you're equipped with a flats boat, one or two 10-weight rods with lots of backing, and a good selection of flies, your best bet is to hire a guide to show you where and how it's done. And the ability to make long, accurate casts couldn't hurt.

Established tarpon flies include the Cockroach Tarpon Fly (TP), the Orange Grizzly TP, the QT Tarpon Shrimp Gurgler, the Silver King fly in black and red,

The real peanut bunker.

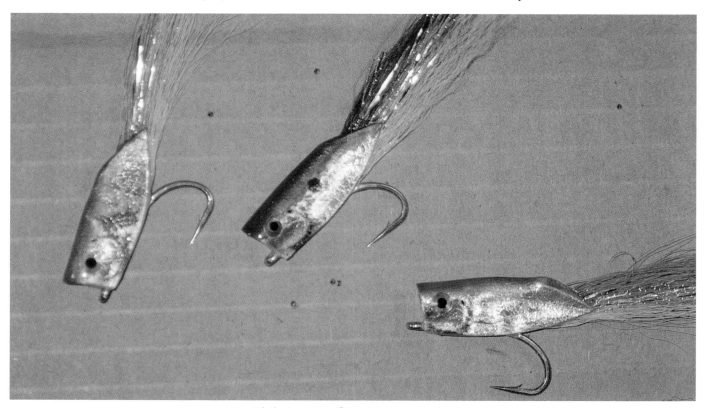

Joe Blados's Crease fly imitates peanut bunker.

earth-tone, or olive, and a large collection of splayed tarpon flies. Tarpon flies are big, usually tied on 1/0 to 3/0 hooks.

GLASS MINNOWS

Baitfish inhabiting the flats are usually composed of several species of small fish. Even though they are diminutive, they make up the bulk of the food that ends up in a predator's stomach. The flies imitating these baitfish are all called glass minnows or candy minnows, because most of the real fish are transparent; the flies are small, flashy, lightweight, and easy to cast. Reflective Mylar provides the main flash, and most of these flies resemble the larger Deceivers, but lightly dressed. All sport hand-painted eyes or just black dots where an eye might be located. There is an entire array of these flies that are identified by their color, including chartreuse, olive, blue-green, brown, and blue-black. There is one called a Glasschovy and even a small Clouser, tied on an up-hook, called the Alba Clouser. Most are tied on 1 or 1/0 stainless steel hooks and range in length from ½ to 1½ inches.

Although most often used on the flats, glass minnows are also an excellent choice in blue water when you're trying to catch bonito or false albacore that have become spooky from seeing too much hardware, large flies, and threatening boats. During their fall visit north, you can't go small enough to catch the Fat Alberts.

The variety in glass minnow designs is almost limitless.

CHAPTER 7

Spinning Gear

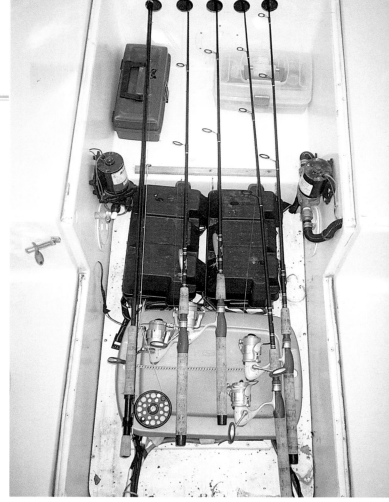

Every boat should be designed with ample rod storage.

Even if you are a devotee of Lefty Kreh, saltwater fly fishing's number-one guru, there are times when the fish are there but weather conditions are against you, making it impossible to get to them with a fly rod. This is when you might want to switch to a spinning outfit. In other sight-fishing situations, the best tackle is determined by the species of fish you are hunting. For example, bottom-feeding fish are often difficult to take with fly-fishing gear because the lure's position on the bottom isn't natural looking in the eyes of a predator fish. When in doubt, carry both kinds of rods and lures.

Fly fishing is both an art and a skill, and it is beyond the capabilities of a small percentage of people (my best estimate, between 5 and 10 percent). These individuals simply lack the coordination needed to fly-fish. Coordination can't be taught or learned; it is the innate ability to use different parts of the body in synchrony, smoothly and efficiently. The skill to cast a fly line depends on timing and an understanding of what is going on behind you without the need to look back. Should people without these skills be denied the pleasure of sight-fishing for bonefish or striped bass because they can't properly present a fly to the fish? I think not. (In my opinion, the de

rigueur use of fly rods by some bonefishermen suffering from a bad case of elitism is unfortunate.) The alternative is to use spinning tackle, which almost everyone can learn to use well enough to catch fish effectively.

Sight-fishing with spinning gear is often defined and touted by apologists as "light-tackle" fishing. However, light tackle has its own inherent flaws. The goal of light-tackle fishing is to wear down a fish to the point where it can be brought back to the boat. A fish too green would destroy light tackle if it were "horsed in." Light tackle is usually defined as line anywhere from 4- to 12-pound-test. Rods are 7 to 8 feet long, often with tips that are on the soft side because the lures are generally small. The drag on the reel is set well below the breaking point of the line, which often entails a drawn-out battle of run and retrieve, run and retrieve, until the fish is exhausted.

Light-tackle fishing is not conducive to the catch-and-release philosophy, however. The purpose behind catch-and-release is to let the fish go so that it can live to be caught again. In reality, it doesn't quite work that way. In a drawn-out battle using light tackle, the fish can't get enough water over its gills to replace the oxygen consumed during the fight. In addition, most fish close their

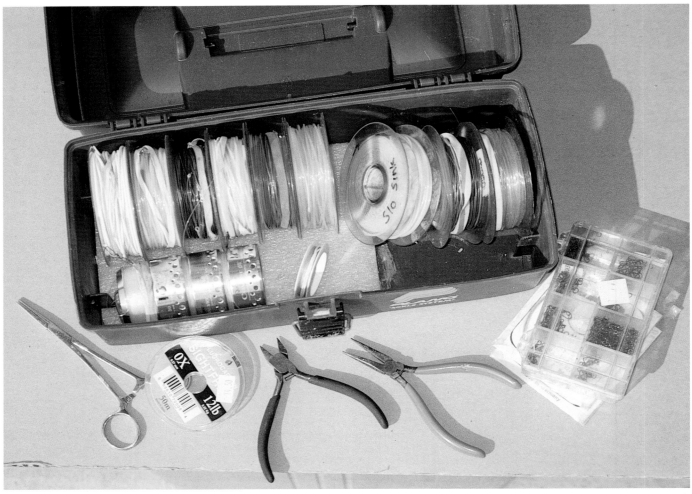

Every boat should have a fully stocked fly toolbox.

gill covers while engaged in this battle, further reducing the water flow. When the fish is released, it might vigorously swim away, making the angler think that the fish is perfectly well. However, the fish is suffering from hypoxia, or oxygen deprivation, and it can't swim fast enough to replace the oxygen lost. Another factor at work is the ambient temperature of the water. The warmer the water, the less dissolved oxygen it contains, making it less likely that the fish can recover. This is a problem in fly fishing as well as spin fishing. So if catch-and-release is your primary goal, use tackle strong enough to overpower the fish, bring it to the boat as quickly as possible, and then release it.

RODS

One feature that spinning tackle has in common with fly-fishing tackle is the flex of the rod. As when selecting a fly rod, a spinning rod with a fast-action tip is preferred. Rod length can vary from 6½ to 8 feet, and the rod should be capable of handling 8- to 15-pound-test monofilament or braided lines. One-piece rods give the angler a greater feel of the lure and the fish, but they are awkward to carry. In most cases, two-piece rods with glass-to-glass ferrules are almost as good.

Rod guides on a spinning rod get a lot more through traffic than do guides on fly rods. Ceramic inserts on the first and preferably the second ring guides are a must, because they are the first to clean the line. Ceramic rings resist line wear better than plain, stainless steel ring guides. A hook minder is also a plus on a spinning rod.

REELS

Most spinning reels on the market today are well made, but the real test of a spinning reel is its drag. Only a few have drags that release at the setting you have established; most must be momentarily pulled at a higher force to get the drag to release. And sometimes, this is just enough force to lose a fish. Those that release immediately usually have a greater number of ball bearings,

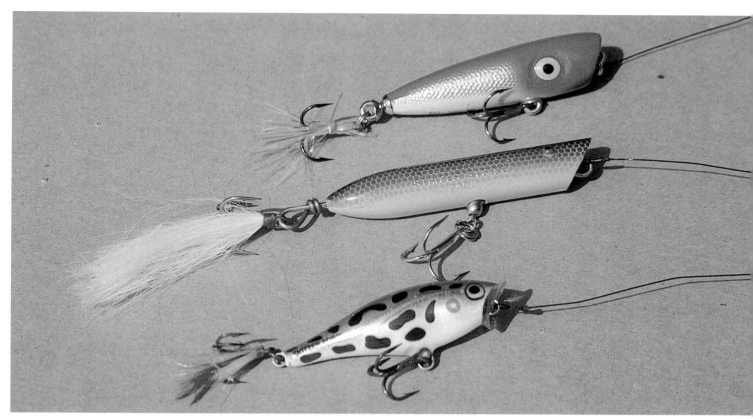

Popping plugs on the flats are a spin fisher's salvation.

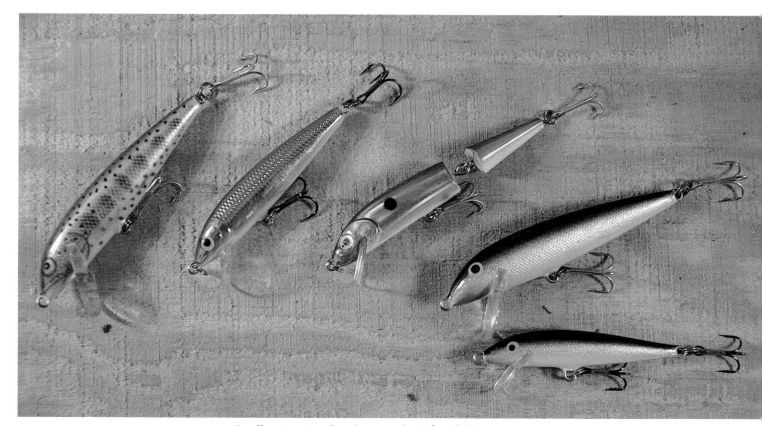

Small swimming plugs have a role in flats fishing.

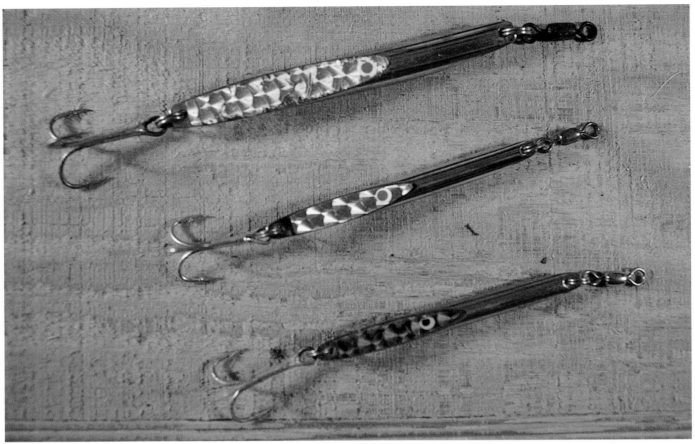

The classic Deadly Dick has become a favorite lure of sight fishers working schools of bonito and false albacore on the edges of the flats.

Small metal lures are often as effective as flies when schools of false albacore push baitfish to the surface.

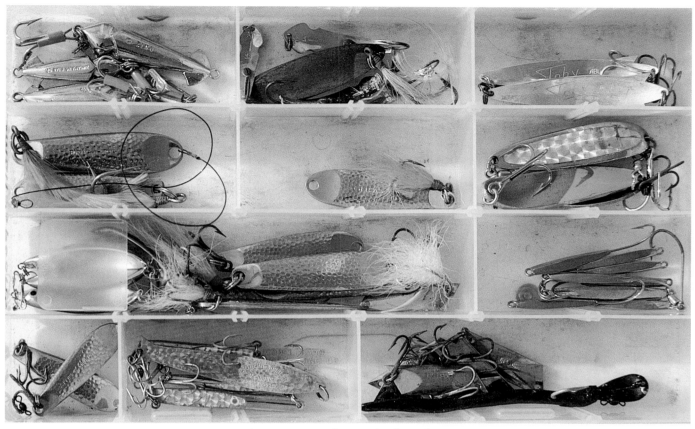

An assortment of proven hardware lures.

which is something you should look for. Of course, make sure you choose a reel that is saltwaterproof.

LINES

Many light-tackle anglers still seem to prefer monofilament lines. However, line diameter is a function of casting distance: the smaller the diameter, the farther a light lure can be tossed. Braided lines are quite a bit thinner than the same pound-test in a monofilament line, and they are especially resistant to abrasion (requiring special scissors to cut them and special knots to tie them). One drawback of braided lines is their limpness. If you're not careful, the line can uncoil of its own accord unless constant pressure is kept on the distal end; usually, the weight of the lure provides enough pressure.

When using monofilament, I load my spools with either 10- or 12-pound-test line. I usually add a 2-foot length of fluorocarbon to the distal end of the working braided or monofilament line, especially if the line's color might alert a fish that something is attached to the lure. Again, to keep the lines light, I add only a snap unless the lure has a tendency to spin. If there are fluke and bluefish in the waters you're fishing, a light, flexible,

dark-colored, braided wire leader, 6 to 10 inches long, is a must.

LURES

Two lure types dominate—popping plugs and subsurface swimming plugs—and both are quite effective. The popping plug in 1½-, 2½-, and 4-inch lengths is effective both on the flats and atop deep water. Preferred color patterns are either green (mackerel) or blue (bluefish). The 3- to 3½-inch jointed, subsurface swimming plug in blue and green patterns is a must, but for some unexplained reason, the rainbow trout pattern is also very effective for striped bass, weakfish, and fluke on the flats. In deeper water, the same jointed plug with a diving plane is a better choice. Striped bass don't really jump (no matter how pretty the decals that show them leaping in the air), but in water less than 2 feet deep, I have had them smash small (2½-inch) surface popping plugs and take them into the air like a tarpon.

Metal lures do have a place in your tackle box, especially when you're after bonito and false albacore. When it comes to sight-fishing, bigger is not always better, especially when using hardware. One reason is that

Tackle box inserts can help organize your onboard inventory.

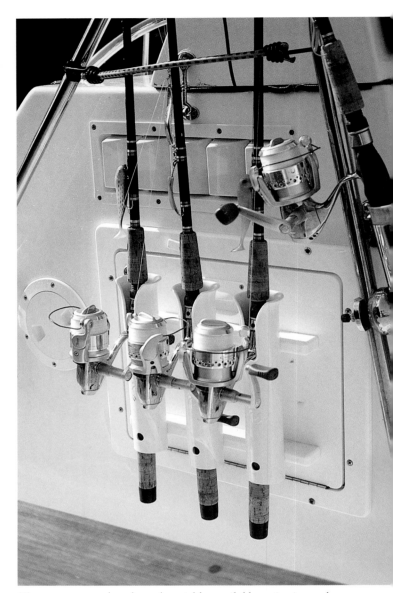

To save space and make rods quickly available, spinning-rod holders can be mounted on tackle box inserts.

bigger metal lures make too much noise and commotion when they hit the water. The small ones are heavy enough to get a decent cast that is far enough away from a traveling school of fish to avoid frightening them. The lures can then be retrieved across the head of the school with great effectiveness. One of the deadliest lures avail-

able to the albacore angler is the Deadly Dick (see chapter 1). Here, you might want to use a snap with a swivel. The old standby, the Hammered Spoon by Hopkins, is also very useful and should be carried in every tackle box. On a par with the Hammered Spoon are Kastmaster Spoons.

CHAPTER 8

Clothing and Accessories

An angler outfitted like this one doesn't belong on a flats boat.

CLOTHING

When it comes to clothing, color is an important consideration. Over the years, I have discovered that two things can make fish wary when an angler comes into view: color and movement. An angler standing on the bow platform can spook the fish if his or her shirt and trousers are bright red, yellow, orange, or blue. In addition, each color has what scientists call a color heat, or color temperature. These bright colors give off a glow that registers with the fish and alerts them to danger.

Colors can create another problem for anglers. For instance, for comfort, the perfect color to wear on a flats boat under the August sun is white—all white. However, this would spook every fish on the flats. Yet if you wore brown, blue, green, or black, you would likely be well done before you saw your first fish or heard the noon whistle blow. Thus, a compromise between your comfort and the fish's fear of bright colors is required. Select

clothing made of tropical tans, pastels such as powder blue, or light shades of green or gray.

Hats. Hats are your first defense against the rays of the sun, and no sight-fishing angler should be without one. Baseball caps or hats with brims are the minimum requirement. If you don't want to be classified as a redneck, you might opt for a hat that has a back cover—like the kind Lefty Kreh or Mark Sosin wears on television. Regardless of the style, pick a hat that is darkly colored on the underside of the brim. If you can't find one, get a can of flat black spray paint, tape the inside of the hat so it doesn't get a dose of paint, and spray two or three coats on the brim. This black underside will reduce much of the reflected glare generated by the sun bouncing off the water. It will also help you concentrate on the view ahead of you.

Shoes. The first consideration is finding a pair of shoes with soles that grip the deck. The material of the soles should not mark the deck of the boat, however (or

Color and movement on the bow can spook fish on the flats. This shirt color is all wrong.

A fore-and-aft hat typically worn by flats fishers in the tropics, where neck protection is a must.

A more traditional hat found on the flats.

If the underside of your hat's brim isn't black, paint it black to reduce the sun's reflection off the water.

Stability on the bow platform starts with a good pair of shoes that grip the deck.

This shirt color is right, and so is the false albacore.

Bow color isn't as crucial in blue water as it is on skinny water.

Left: This shirt color is acceptable. Right: Cold-weather rain gear is a must at the beginning and end of the fishing season in northern climes. Although wearing yellow on the bow can be a problem, it is less critical on the poling platform.

you may have to answer to the person behind the wheel). Canvas shoes are fine, and getting them wet is never a concern. Leather shoes often fit better because of their inherent rigidity, but they can get hot and are negatively affected by salt or rainwater. If you choose leather shoes, make sure they have breathing ports.

Shirts. Loose-fitting, short-sleeved shirts made of modern synthetic fabrics are almost the standard uniform for flats and blue-water anglers afloat from June to late September. These shirts, originally designed for tropical anglers, are ventilated and cool, they dry quickly if you're caught in a squall, and they always look good because they're wrinkle free. But early and late in the fishing season—from April to June and again in October and November—anglers switch to long-sleeved cotton shirts. If the weather turns warm unexpectedly, most of these stylish shirts come equipped with a button and a flap so that the sleeve can be rolled up and anchored in that position. Alternatively, when the weather cools, syn-

thetic shirts can be layered with silk or cotton turtleneck shirts.

Trousers. Like shirts, today's trouser fabrics provide ventilation and dry quickly when wet. They are often equipped with cargo pockets and usually have button-locked rear pockets that keep your wallet in your pants and not afloat.

Shorts. Unless you're plagued with alabaster skin or the weather is too cool, you'll probably opt to wear shorts when on a flats boat. Avoid Bermuda shorts or long, baggy shorts that cramp your knees when you bend. Short shorts—with a 6- to 9-inch inseam—will keep you comfortable in even the hottest weather.

Foul-weather gear. For fishing early or late in the season, there is foul-weather gear that can make you immune to the elements; however, it is heavy and cumbersome. For most of the fishing season, you can go considerably lighter, fishing in the rain with just a simple plastic poncho with a hood. More effective than the poncho is a two-piece rain suit. The hoods on these suits are usually better fitting than those on ponchos, with drawstrings that can be tied tightly to keep you dry. Choose a rain suit with pants that are held up by suspenders rather than a waist cord. The suspendered bottoms allow better air circulation, and there is less chance for moisture to become trapped inside. Good rain gear not only protects you from getting wet but also acts as a windbreaker, hoarding your body heat and limiting evaporation on your skin, which can lower your body temperature.

Color is also a consideration in the rain gear you choose. If you're going to be in the bow of the boat, avoid yellow- or orange-colored rain gear. Darker colors are better if you can't find anything in a light tan or gray. You might be able to get away with yellow rain gear if you're on the poling platform.

EYEWEAR

Obviously, when sight-fishing, your eyesight is all-important. The sun can be either your best friend or your worst enemy. You must learn to use it to your advantage and guard against its harmful rays. Your first line of defense against the sun is a quality pair of sunglasses. Although regular lenses made of plastic or glass will help, they don't compare with the glare-reduction ability of polarized lenses. Fortunately, many inexpensive, over-the-counter sunglasses are made with Polaroid filters. If they aren't labeled as such, it's easy to determine for yourself whether the lenses are polarized: Hold them at arm's length and look out in the direction of the sun (but never directly at it). Rotate the glasses 90 degrees either left or right, and if the glare from the sun disappears and then reappears when rotated back, they are polarized lenses.

Polaroid lenses eliminate much of the reflected glare emanating from the water's surface and thus increase

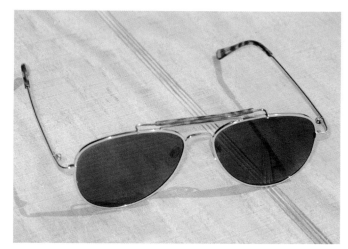

Store-bought Polaroids work if you don't need prescription lenses.

Store-bought wraparounds are a better choice.

Snap-on glasses are a quick fix for sun on the flats.

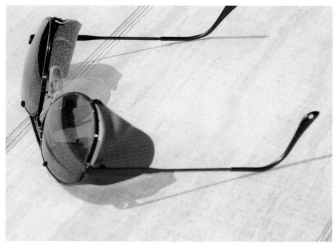

If you need prescription sunglasses, choose a pair with side shields to block out stray rays.

your ability to see what is in the water. The Polaroid lens does this by polarizing, or filtering, some of the sun's rays. It restricts the light's transverse wave vibrations and allows only vertical light to pass through the lens and reach your eyes.

If you wear prescription glasses, you can buy snap-on Polaroids. A better idea is to get a pair of prescription Polaroids. You can even send your prescription to one of several outfitters that produce Polaroid glasses with hinged, leather side blinders, often called wraparound glasses. Stray sunlight entering from the side reduces the effectiveness of polarized glasses because this light doesn't pass through the filtering lenses. Wraparound sunglasses offer you the ultimate in water visibility.

Lens color. Two lens colors, amber and gray, are available. Although both are valuable to anglers bent on sight-fishing, the choice between them depends on the fishing environment. Experience and usage have shown that inshore sight fishers can better see what is in the water through amber-colored lenses. Amber affects the color of objects seen, tending to make fish appear darker in contrast to the bottom. Finding fish in the water is difficult anyway, because their natural coloration camouflages them to some degree. Actually, what you see first is the shadow of the fish on the bottom; then you spot the fish above it. Amber-colored lenses also have a better light-gathering ability than gray lenses do. This is substantiated by hunters who don such lenses after the sun goes down or on overcast days, when the light begins to fade.

The opposite is true for offshore or off-the-flats sight fishers. Gray is a neutral color (actually, it's not a color at all) and therefore doesn't alter the color of the light. Here, gray lenses perform better to combat the greater reflective ability of these waters because they block more of the sun's unwanted light.

Plastic versus glass lenses. This can be a difficult decision. Plastic lenses are lightweight and can be worn all day without irritating the bridge of your nose. However, they are more susceptible to scratching unless you take proper care of them and put them in a case whenever you're not wearing them. You can get plastic lenses with an antiscratch finish, but it's not totally scratch proof. Glass lenses are heavier than plastic, especially when side blinders are added. Unless they fit perfectly, they can become irritating after a long day in the sun. The choice is a personal one.

OTHER NECESSITIES
Food and Beverages
If you are hungry or thirsty, you won't be able to give the fish your full concentration. When determining how much food and water to bring, you should always assume that you'll be afloat for longer than planned. The water factor can be very important on hot summer days. I always carry an emergency food kit on my boats that includes bottled water, an assortment of granola bars and the like, and a bag or two of trail mix. Don't pack anything salty unless you have an unlimited supply of beverages. These foods are not designed to fully satisfy your hunger but only to hold you over until you get back to port. There is no place for alcohol on a sight-fishing boat.

Logbook
A logbook is a diary of what you see from your boat and what you accomplish each day you're afloat. The data you record in it can be an invaluable resource in the future. It is your fishing history and a measure of your success or the lack thereof, and it will allow you to learn from your mistakes if you accurately enter everything that happens. Some of the data should be entered while you are afloat and then fully documented later that day or at night over a cup of coffee. Be sure to make all your entries in permanent ink, because in all probability, the logbook will get wet from time to time.

The best logbooks are bound, hardcover books with blank pages measuring about 5½ by 9 inches—small enough to easily fit into a jacket pocket. You can enter all the data each day by hand, or to save some time, you can go to a stationery store and have rubber stamps made for all the data headings you need. You can even set up a logbook page, with all your data headings, on your computer and then take it to a printer to have logbooks printed and bound. I had two dozen such logbooks made and was surprised at how little it cost.

The first of your data headings should consist of the date, the port from which you sailed that day, and the engine hours (from the engine's gauge) at both the beginning and the end of the day. If you are operating an inboard engine, you should also have a check box showing that you checked the fuel, oil, coolant, battery, and transmission fluid levels.

The next logbook entry is the crew on board or the names of the people who fished with you that day. Also important is the climatic data, including sky conditions (rain, fog, sun), air temperature, and several water temperatures, starting with the one at the dock inside the marina, another one when you get outside the marina, and one at the end of the day. Before you leave the dock, note the state of the tide (flooding or ebbing) and when the next high and low tides are scheduled to occur. Equally important is the wind, both its direction and its estimated velocity. Next comes an entry for sea

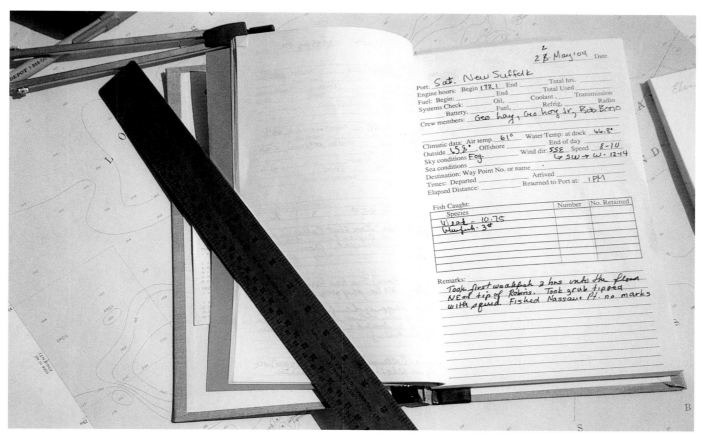

A well-kept logbook can be the key to successful future fishing.

conditions, such as flat or slight chop, and wave heights. You may also want to log your intended destination and describe where you fished and when you returned to port. Under another heading, list the species of fish you caught, their size (weight or length), and the number released. At the end of these data entries, leave several lines under the heading "Remarks." This should be your analysis of the day's fishing.

From this logbook data, you can predict what to expect on the same day in subsequent years. After several years of averaging your accumulated data, these predictions will become progressively more accurate. Conditions won't always be exactly the same, of course, but for some variables such as water temperature, they probably won't be off by more than a few degrees unless you're hit by some exceptional weather. The logbook is one of your best tools for predicting future success. Guard it from your competition, and make sure to complete it every day. Don't leave home or the boat without it.

Cell Phone

Another item that you shouldn't leave home without is a cell phone. There was a time in the not too distant past when you could quickly reach a marine operator on one or two channels of your VHF radio. This is no longer the case. Local telephone companies once had operators standing by around the clock to aid mariners, but cost-cutting practices have all but eliminated this service. If someone on your boat has a medical emergency, the cell phone is the quickest way to ensure that help will come to you or be there to meet you at the dock. The Coast Guard still diligently monitors Channel 16, but that should be your call of last resort. The station responding is probably far away and will have to contact the local police or emergency medical services, which might result in a delay. Use your cell phone when time is of the essence.

VHF and CB Radios

Every boat should have a VHF marine radio—even a small flats boat. These radios are now so small that they can be tucked away almost anywhere on your craft. In addition, small sailboat whips (antennae), with knock-down capabilities, can be placed on a flats boat in an out-of-the-way location and turned vertical only when you need them.

Citizens band (CB) radio use has changed drastically in the past few decades. Twenty-five years ago, almost

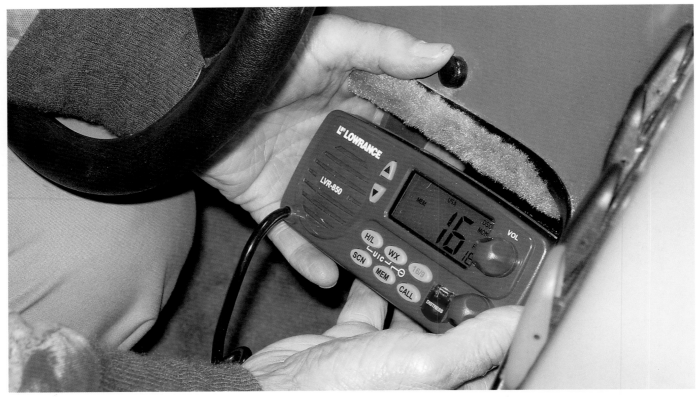

Today's VHF radio are small and efficient. Don't leave the dock without one.

every boat had one because they were far less expensive than VHF radios. Some larger boats had both. The demise of the CB radio was caused in part by the constant chatter and clutter on them, especially by those who illegally increased their power and thus their range, blasting others off the air. Today, even eighteen-wheeler operators seldom use their CB sets.

The cell phone was another cause of the CB's demise—but that's a plus. Because of their limited range of 5 to 10 miles or so, they keep the talk localized. A few smart boaters—often fishing club members who fish the same area and like to keep in touch with one another—have sneaked small, relatively inexpensive CB radios onto their boats. To keep the crowd small, they don't broadcast what they've done. And the new CB models have lots of improved features. So if you want to be in contact with your buddies but don't want to broadcast your position over VHF Channel 6 (the channel assigned to marine-to-marine communications), get a CB set.

First-Aid Kit

Another item that should be in every flats boat is a complete first-aid kit. Some kits are specially designed to be carried on boats and come in waterproof boxes that snap tightly shut and can be stored in small compartments. Not included are dehooking kits—a real must on a fish-

ing boat. Add to these items a small can of anesthetic spray such as Solarcaine to alleviate the pain of those fair-skinned anglers who forgot sunscreen and didn't bring a long-sleeved shirt.

Binoculars

Binoculars come in several styles. Marine binoculars are specifically built to withstand the rigors of a saltwater environment, and many can float if accidentally knocked into the water. Another useful feature is a fixed focus with a depth of field so great that most faraway objects are already in focus. This is helpful if several people use a pair of binoculars, avoiding the need to set a different focus for each individual. Some binoculars are designed to be used if you wear glasses; they compensate for the added distance from eye to the first lens, so you don't have to take off your glasses every time you look through the binoculars. A well-equipped dealer in marine supplies should have several models for you to consider.

Tools and Such

Pliers. No one is ready to fish without a pair of needle-nose pliers strapped in a holster on one side of his or her belt; on the other side should be a cased jackknife. Both items are indispensable during a day on the water. The needle-nose pliers can save a lot of cut fingers when

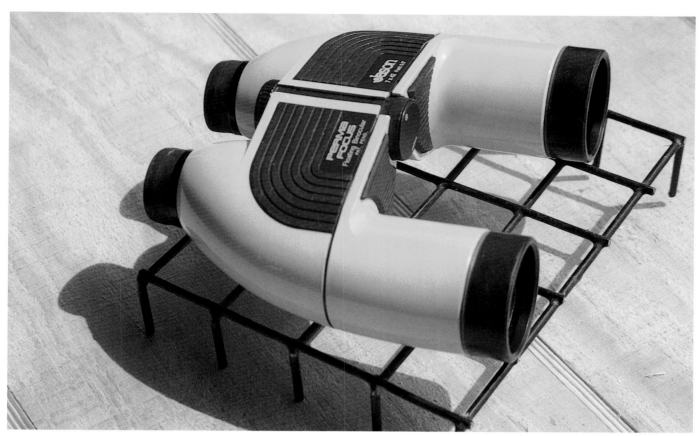

Floating binoculars.

Waterproof binoculars.

Ideal storage rack for binoculars while you're fishing.

Tools for the compleat sight fisher. From left to right: case and long-bladed knife, needle-nose pliers with side cutter (top) and bottom side-cutting pliers, and line snippers with lanyard.

you're trying to reverse a hook in the mouth of a toothy bluefish or barracuda. The choice between short- and long-nose pliers is a personal one. There is also one manufacturer that sells a variety of holsters for holding all kinds of implements on your belt. One comes equipped with a pouch to hold a small pair of diagonal pliers perfect for cutting monofilament tags.

Nail clippers. If you come upon a dedicated flats fisher, you are almost guaranteed to see a pair of nail clippers dangling from a lanyard around his or her neck. They are invaluable whether you are a fly fisher or a spin fisher. I don't wear mine around my neck because they tangle with the strap that holds my reading glasses. Instead, I loop the lanyard around a screw eye at the edge of the boat's windshield. Located there, the nail clippers are ready to use by anyone fishing with me.

Reading (magnifying) glasses. Even though you might not need them for reading the fine print, reading glasses are invaluable when you need to trim flies, tie small knots, or thread a line through a size 12 fly's eye. Cheap reading glasses are sold in almost every pharmacy for less than $12. You can even find glasses that actually magnify what you look at through them.

PART III

The Fishing

Now that you have some knowledge as to what makes a predator fish hunt and have amassed the necessary equipment, from boats to lures and everything in between, it is time to get out there and test your gear along with your fishing skills.

If you have done your homework, you should already have some idea of where to hunt for predator fish on the flats nearest to home. The key to successful predator fishing is making the best use of the equipment available to you. You must also realize that sight fishing is a learning process and it is important to take advantage of all the techniques that have been developed for the sport. However, experience is still the greatest learning tool there is. The more you practice these techniques, the more likely you will be to catch fish.

Even small bass can be a challenge to catch on a fly rod.

CHAPTER 9

Where and How to Look for Fish

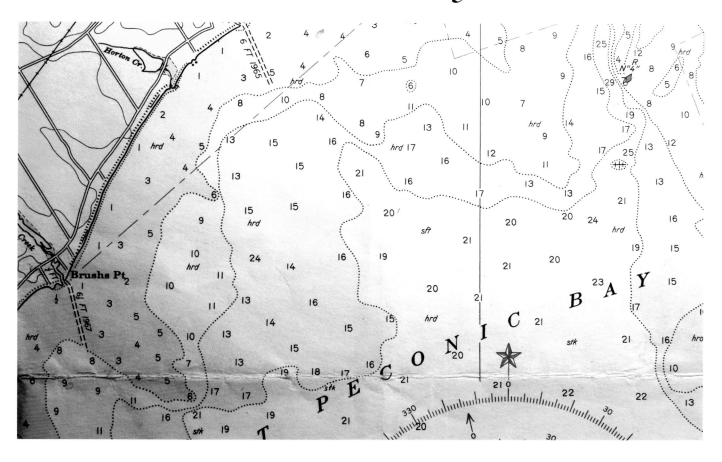

Even before you leave home, you should have some idea where to start your search for fish. It's a big ocean out there, and narrowing your focus is the first step.

NAUTICAL CHARTS

Nautical charts (available at your local tackle shop or boat dealer) can be your best friend if you know how to read them correctly. They can help you avoid a lot of fruitless wandering in areas where sight fishing is unlikely or impossible. Interpreting the information on a nautical chart is simple. The symbols are self-explanatory, and the four colors—yellow, green, blue, and white—denote the following: Yellow is dry land, and green identifies wet or swampy land; green can also indicate breeding grounds for fish if they have an outlet (a stream) into salt water. Blue denotes water, and some charts may use two shades—dark blue for shallower water, and light blue for deeper water (the opposite of what one would assume intuitively). White denotes deep water.

Sight fishers should be interested only in the darker blue areas, because that's where the water depth won't interfere with visibility. The two blue colors are separated by dotted lines—called contour lines—and their shape tells you what the shape of the bottom is like. The first contour line separating dark blue from light blue is the 1-fathom line (a fathom is equivalent to 6 feet). The second contour line in the light blue is the 2-fathom (or 12-foot) line, the next contour line is the 3-fathom (or 18-foot) line, and so on. Beyond the 18-fathom line, the water is shown as white on the chart.

Top: On nautical charts, the shade of blue changes as the water depth increases.

All the numbers scattered in the water on a nautical chart indicate the water's depth in feet. Both these depths and the contour lines indicate the depth at mean low water, or low tide. The depth of the water gradually increases above these numbers as the tide floods. The reverse is also true, unless there is an unusual weather phenomenon at work that temporarily keeps the depth from getting lower—this is usually the kind of weather you want to avoid when fishing.

While still at home, make note—both on the chart and in your mind—where the potential sight-fishing sites might be. Then, armed with the chart and at low tide, take your boat out and begin cruising the flats, bays, or rivers in your area. In some places, the inner 6-foot zone can vary in width from a few feet to a mile or more, and it may be several miles long. In one place where I fish, the flat averages three-quarters of a mile wide and is 9 miles long. That gives me an unbelievable 4,480 acres of flats to search. And even with a pair of electric motors on the boat, this can involve a lot of cruising.

SEABIRDS

There is one natural aid that can help you narrow down the search area and get to the fish quickly: seabirds. Two types of seabirds, terns and gulls, can be useful for locating fish. Terns, however, are less desirable, because they tend to go crazy—diving and screaming—over nothing. Gulls, in contrast, are serious when they start yelling. It means that a school of baitfish is being eaten from underneath by predator fish. As pieces of chopped fish float to the surface, the gulls are there to take advantage of the feast—and to tell you where the predators are dining.

Finding gulls is not always an easy task. Many of them seem to be spending inordinate amounts of time at municipal dumps rather than hunting on the water. If you do find birds diving and feeding a long way off, it's best to scan them with a set of binoculars to determine what's really going on. This can mean the difference between taking a 1- or 2-mile run and finding fish and making a wasted run that gets you to the site after all the action is over.

HOW TO INTERPRET WHAT YOU SEE

When you look into the water, things are not always where they appear to be. Interpreting the underwater world can be confusing, and it takes experience to become proficient at it. However, the following information may help you understand what is happening.

Angle of incidence and angle of reflection. This may be more physics than you care to know, but it will help you better understand why the fish can see you before you see them, and why they aren't really where you think they are. The reason is that you seldom see sunlight enter the water at a right (90-degree) angle, even at high noon. The angle at which the light enters the water is called the angle of incidence (AI), and the angle at which it leaves the water's surface, heading away from you, is called the angle of reflection (AR). Both angles are always equal. All rays entering the water at angles greater than 90 degrees are totally reflected.

Gulls blitz as predators from beneath attack a school of baitfish.

A gull waits for his buddies to find a predator fish attack.

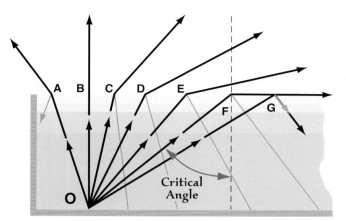

All rays entering the water at angles greater than the critical angle are completely reflected.

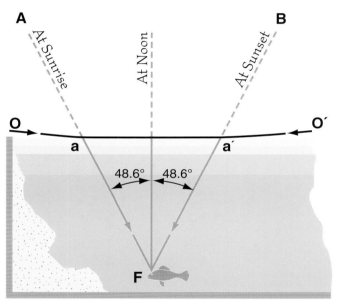

Angle of refraction. The fish sees the image of the sun along AF.

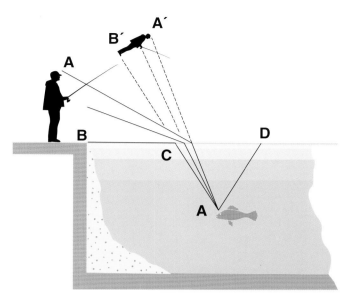

The fish sees the fisherman "up in the air."

Angle of refraction. The angle of refraction is what causes you to think you see an object at a place different from its actual location. When a beam of light enters the water, some of it is not reflected in the exact opposite direction; a portion enters the water and is refracted, or bent, thus changing its direction. This is caused by the difference in the densities of the mediums through which the beam passes—that is, it travels from an environment of light density, the air, to one of a greater density, the water.

The angle of refraction is never as large as the angle of incidence, because some of the sun's rays penetrate the surface and enter the water. However, the angle at which these rays travel in the water is not a straight-line extension (180 degrees) of the angle of incidence; because the change in density causes the light ray to bend, the angle of refraction is always less than 180 degrees. The lower the sun is on the horizon, the greater the refraction; therefore, late in the day, a fish in the water appears to be closer than if you saw the same fish at noon.

What the fish see. To better understand the fish you're after, it may help to look at the world above the water's surface from the fish's perspective. The sun's height above the horizon is constantly changing as it moves from east to west across the sky. At sunrise, the incident light from the sun is refracted (bent) downward as it enters the water. At this time, because the image of the sun is bent, the fish can actually see below the horizon. Only when the sun is straight up, at 90 degrees, does the fish see the sun where it actually is.

In the accompanying figure, 0 to 0' represents the smooth, unruffled surface of a tidal pond. At sunrise, the incident light is at *a* on the pond's surface, but as it enters the water, it is refracted downward and reaches the eye of the fish, making it appear to the fish that the sun is high in the heavens. As the sun travels across the sky, its apparent motion is through the smaller angle AFB.

Also consider the appearance of the fisherman as he is viewed by the fish in the next figure. Although he is standing at the water's edge, the man's image seems to be higher in the air at A'B'. As a result, he spooks the fish before he can even see it.

CHAPTER 10

The Perfect Sight-Fishing Day

Perfect conditions for sight fishing don't occur with any regularity. Therefore, to be successful, you must be able to compensate for the lack of perfection. A perfect day has only three requirements: a bright sun in a cloudless sky, a falling tide (with 1 to 4 feet of water between your boat and the bottom), and no wind. How Mother Nature manipulates any of these factors can make the difference between a great day and a dismal day.

SUN

The direction from which the sunlight is emanating determines where you can and cannot sight-fish. Because of visibility requirements, you must have the sun at your back. In any other position, the sun's reflection off the water will blind you.

During the flats-fishing season, the sun shines from the southeast quadrant before noon. One of the nice things about flats fishing from mid-April to the end of June is that you don't need to get up early to catch a fish. In fact, I seldom start fishing before 9 a.m. Even though the sun may rise at around 4 a.m., I don't push off for another five hours or so because I need the sun to illuminate the bottom. I'm not looking for the fish per se but for their shadows, which are much easier to spot. Striped bass and weakfish—two species I usually look for this time of year—are difficult if not impossible to see on a sandy, tan-colored bottom. And if the fish have been on the flats for a week or more, their body color gets even lighter, and their heads and tails seem to disappear.

Top: A beach at low tide reveals a barricade of boulders.

Beach wind this strong means no boats on the flats.

The only time you can see the actual fish is when they're moving, and if they're moving, they've been spooked. Therefore, the sun must be high enough in the sky for the fish to cast shadows. Then, you can gauge the distance between their bodies and their shadows.

TIDES

The state of the tide—how high or low it is—strongly affects how well you can see into the water column. The higher the tide, the less visibility there is. Thus, a perfect day on the flats has a falling tide that is at least halfway through its cycle. Visibility gets better as the tide continues to falls, but if the water gets too shallow, the fish will move out.

Tidal flow in the spring and early summer also affects the water temperature on the flats. On a sunny day, water temperature is elevated by exposure to sunlight. If the bottom is muddy or dark, the heat absorption by the water is even greater. In the early part of the season, that's a plus, but toward the end, it can negatively affect the fish's activity. Striped bass, for example, can't

tolerate water temperatures above 71 degrees. So if you want to catch bass, you'll have to wait an hour or two after the tide turns and it begins to flood, bringing in cooler water from the nearby depths—and bringing in the bass with it.

WIND AND RAIN

Wind is probably the single most influential factor when it comes to seeing what is in the water. It can ruin an otherwise favorable day because there is no way to compensate for its effects. Even a slight dimpling on the water can make it difficult to see under the surface, and anything stronger can make it impossible.

Don't despair. Although there's nothing you can do to change the way the wind blows, there are two things you can do to avoid it. The first is to fish early in the day. The sun acts as a wind generator, so it may take an hour or two after sunrise for it to really start blowing. Of course, the visibility won't be great, but you might still be able to pick out a fish or two. The second way is to fish the leeward side of an island or a flat under a high bluff of land that blocks the wind. Although the fishable area won't be as wide as you might like, it is a workable alternative.

Almost as bad as wind is rain. It mars the water's surface and, of course, it rains only when there are clouds in the sky. When wind and rain occur together, they constitute weather. Weather fronts are predictable, however. You can learn to read and interpret the sky, looking for the kinds of clouds that precede a front, or you can keep your eye on a barometer—when the pressure plummets, bad weather is in the offing. You can also listen to twenty-four-hour weather forecasts on the radio. But because forecasts may not be tailored to your particular area, it's to your benefit to be able to read weather signs in advance.

You don't have to be a meteorologist to know that clouds like these may mean a day at the dock.

CHAPTER 11

Fishing the Mini-Flats

There are really two kinds of flats. More common are the wide, shallow flats with a minimal tidal current and a fairly uniform depth. Then there are the abbreviated or mini-flats, which have some of the characteristics of traditional flats as well as a few of their own. Mini-flats are usually found bordering islands or points of land and are excellent locations to practice sight fishing. As the term denotes, they are not very wide but can be quite long. The feature that makes them so narrow is the presence of deep water close by. Thus, a boat might be in 10 feet or more of water, but the sight fisher is still working the shallows along the beach. In mini-flats, the ideal sight depth—6 inches to 3 or 4 feet—may be just 5 to 10 feet wide before the bottom disappears into the depths. Also, the incline from the beach to deeper water can be steep.

Compensating for the smaller area of mini-flats is the fact that the nearby depths often hold predator fish that always keep at least one eye focused on the beach and the skinny water leading to it. This might necessitate some of blind casting, because the predator fish aren't always in the shallows. However, they are quick to note anything entering the shallow water, which means that poppers or bass bugs—anything that creates a disturbance—can be very effective.

RIPS, HEAVY FLOWS, AND POINTS OF LAND

Mini-flats aren't always continuous along the beach; they are often interrupted by points of land that jut immediately into deep water. Tidal currents passing these points of land cause rips to form. These rips hold a lot of baitfish and make them easy prey for predator fish. The

Top: From the angle of the sloping beach, you can predict that the mini-flat under the water is also short and steep.

Fish the down-current side of boulders on the flats, and don't mind the seals.

This wide rip tells you that the fish are just ahead of the turbulent water.

currents often disrupt the integrity of a school of bait-fish, so they are easily singled out as food for the predators. Often, the baitfish rise to the surface to escape, and feeding blitzes may occur. Most of the time, however, the action takes place under the water's surface, and it is here where sight fishers can find fish.

BOULDERS, GROINS, JETTIES, AND DOCKS

In some respects, sight fishing has parallels to black bass fishing on freshwater lakes or rivers, where the fish take advantage of man-made structures. Around many islands and along coastal beaches in areas that have been glaciated, boulders of all sizes were washed out of the soil by centuries of rain and storm waves pounding the line where land and water met. These rows of boulders in the water, often just a few feet off the beach, offer some good mini-flats fishing. Here, skillful sight fishers can spot predator fish, often on the down-current side, waiting for the tide to sweep food into their realm.

Elsewhere along the beach, where glacial deposition has not taken place, human beings have stepped in to control beach erosion with numerous groins built of riprap (quarried stones) or stone jetties to reduce the wave action in a harbor or to protect a harbor entrance. These are excellent places to sight-fish, because baitfish often find protection in the pockets of water created by the irregularly mined rocks. Predator fish know this and can often be spotted just off the rocks waiting for food to come out. Don't pass up a jetty or groin, and fish both up- and down-tide sections.

Surprisingly, many baitfish as well as predator fish like to hang around docks or even bridge abutments. Tidal currents passing through such man-made structures cause eddies to form on the down-tide side, and these are great place to search for predator fish.

LEARNING ON OTHER ANGLERS

In today's world, you rarely find yourself alone on productive sight-fishing flats. Some of the other anglers there are licensed guides who do it as a business; the remainder are there strictly for the sport and the challenge. Don't make the mistake of looking at either group as competition. Instead, look at them as valuable sources of information and know-how. If you watch them and incorporate their suc-

cessful techniques into your own repertoire, you will surely enhance your sight-fishing skills. This has been described as "learning on other fishermen."

To do this, you must be a keen, unobtrusive observer—*unobtrusive* being the key word. You must respect other anglers on the beach and on the water. The best way to avoid any territorial infringement is to stop your boat and watch from a distance. This

Don't crowd anglers on the beach, who aren't as fortunate as you in your boat.

LEARNING ON OTHER ANGLERS

can be facilitated with a pair of good binoculars, 10X or better in power. With such equipment, the other angler may even be unaware of your interest.

The primary information you gather from other anglers on the flats is where they are fishing. Ask yourself, what is unique about this spot compared with adjacent waters? Do you know of similar environments elsewhere? How deep is the water? What species of fish is the angler after? Is he or she spinning or fly-fishing? Have you see the angler fighting a fish? Even if you haven't, don't discount the spot. Maybe the fish just haven't moved in yet. Or there may be other factors affecting the catching of fish. Don't trust your memory; jot down all the pertinent data in your logbook. If you have a camera with a long lens, take a photograph of the area to remind yourself what it looks like. You might be able to spot a unique environmental characteristic in a photograph that you couldn't see in person.

Don't pass too close to other anglers on the flats. Sometimes this can't be avoided, but don't slow your speed unless it's excessive. Never stop and ask other anglers how they're doing, even if you know them. Simply tip your hat or give a slight wave and keep on going. But do note in your logbook that Captain Joe Blow was fishing off Piney Point and it looked like he might have been into fish.

Guides may not always respect one another, but you'll never find them bunching up or fishing close together on the flats (except perhaps on blue water where they've found a school of feeding albies). But many recreational anglers have a tendency to gather in a bunch, especially if one is spotted fighting a fish. Don't join such a crowd, even if you're desperate to catch a fish. Instead, note in your logbook where the place is, what time you were there, and the state of the tide. In a sense, all those anglers are helping you locate fish. You might try that spot the following day, getting there earlier to beat the crowd. Or, if you pass that spot again on the way back to the dock and the boats are gone, go inside just to check out the water depth and temperature and the bottom composition. You might even discover that the crowd didn't catch all the fish.

Don't crowd other boat anglers, especially to see what they've hooked.

CHAPTER 12

Tidal Pond Tactics

T he essence of successful sight fishing is locating fish that you can see and cast to. Knowing that a tidal pond outlet encourages the concentration of predator fish can be valuable information and a major method of finding these fish, but it is useful only for two to three months in the spring.

WHAT IS A TIDAL POND?
A tidal pond is a shallow depression in the land near a body of salt water; its bottom is below mean low tide, and the pond's opening has access to outside waters. Because of the gravitational force of the water's weight and the added effects of the sun's and moon's gravity on the earth's waters, every six hours or so these tidal ponds fill (flood) and then drain (ebb) with salt water from the outside.

Tidal ponds occur naturally and are the result of two geological phenomena: glaciation, especially along the

northeastern coast of the United States, and land erosion on a mountainous scale, along the West, East, and Gulf coasts. Tidal ponds are in a constant state of construction and demolition. The rate is so slow, however, that most anglers don't notice any change in their lifetimes.

The process began 20,000 years ago when temperatures in the atmosphere north and south of the equator began to rise. This caused the great northern continental ice cap to start to melt. Because it melted first at its most southerly extremes, to many observers it appeared to be retreating. However, glaciers can move in only one direction—south (north of the equator)—and only when they are forming. When life is over for them, they simply melt. Twenty thousand years ago, the ocean levels were about 400 feet below where they are today. As

Top: Dam Pond, a typical tidal pond on the North Fork of Long Island, New York.

89

melting began, the oceans rose. When they rose high enough, their landward edges met the terminal moraines left by the glacier's farthest trek south. On the continental shelf, this moraine extends from Manhattan to Cape Cod. In the coastal waters south of the New York bight, massive erosion of the Appalachian Mountains carried mud, sand, gravel, and debris as the highlands were worn down by rain and frost over eons. This action formed a vast alluvial plain between the eastern base of the mountains and the edge of the Atlantic continental shelf. As the ocean continued to rise, it began to slowly fill the shallower depressions along the coast with salt water. At this point, whenever the diurnal tide flowed, the water found a way in and then out, creating an outlet for these ponds. Over the last 20,000 years, the ocean has continued to rise. As a result, some tidal ponds were eventually inundated and destroyed, while farther up the beach (northward) and westward along the coastline, new tidal ponds were created.

WHY DO TIDAL PONDS ATTRACT FISH?

For the most part, tidal ponds are shallow, ranging from as little as 2 to 3 feet deep at low tide to as much as 12 feet deep. Some tidal ponds never drain totally, and these have the greatest potential for attracting fish. In general, the shallower the tidal pond, the greater its attracting mechanism; however, deeper tidal ponds usually have shoal areas that help create this attracting mechanism—which is heat.

The only source of heat in these environments is the sun. Over years upon years of vegetation growth and death, the original white, sandy bottom of the pond becomes darkened by humus (decomposed leaves, grasses, and other plant material) and mud. Fortunately, most of this debris settles to the bottom and isn't washed out of the pond each time the tide moves out. The dark bottom of the pond absorbs sunlight and transfers this warmth to the water above it. When this warmed water begins to ebb out of the pond into the cooler bay water, the pond water's lack of miscibility holds it together. Because the heated pond water has a slightly different density than the surrounding water, it tends to act like a river—or, more appropriately, a stream or a creek. It can travel for miles into the main body of water before it becomes diluted. Fish, acutely attuned to water temperature, sense this warm water and follow it to its source, much like a homing beacon.

In addition to the heat, predator fish are attracted by the smell of food carried from the pond out into the current. A pond's humus bottom produces an abundance of microorganisms, which in turn attract small, maturing fish and crustaceans that feed on them. Also, stands of marine grasses in the pond act as nurseries for these baitfish, providing protection as well as food until they are big enough to cope with predator fish outside their home pond. In addition, other baitfish that do not call the pond home enter with the flooding tide, searching for fish and crustaceans, and then move out when the tide ebbs.

HOW TO FIND TIDAL PONDS

The first step in finding tidal ponds is to get a National Oceanic and Atmospheric Administration chart of the area where you fish. Locate all the blue-colored water that parallels the yellow-colored landmasses. This water, inside the contour line, is 3 fathoms (18 feet) at its deepest but dwindles to nothing along the beach. Next, follow the line that demarcates the land area. If you find small, light-blue colored areas (the same color as the outside water) circled by a thin black line, you've found a pond. But is it a tidal pond? If it has an attached inlet or outlet that connects to the outside water, chances are good that it is a tidal pond. However, in some cases, the channels draining ponds may be so small that the cartographer considered them too insignificant to include on the map.

The next step is to get out in your boat and check each tidal pond visually. Be sure to carry a digital camera and a notebook to record what you find. I located sixty-two legitimate, working tidal ponds on the chart of my area, and it took more than a few days to visit them all. But in doing so, I developed a long list of potential fishing spots. You might find some ponds that don't have outlets but still seem to fall and rise with the tides. These ponds usually have so little beach between them and the outside water that the pond waters seep through the sand. Forget about these ponds—the fish you're seeking can't make their way through the sand.

WHEN TO FISH TIDAL PONDS

The best time to fish these ponds is when the water is ebbing and baitfish are leaving to avoid being trapped in a waterless hole. But not all ebb tides are created equal. Fishing tidal ponds is successful only when the outside waters are cooler than the exiting pond water. This occurs anywhere from April to the end of June in the Northeast and somewhat earlier in the mid-Atlantic states and the Southeast.

The perfect day to fish a tidal pond is when the tide begins to flood the pond at 8 A.M. By 2 P.M., the current slows. It may take fifteen to thirty minutes before it turns and begins to ebb. The water has been in the pond for six hours, and the heat from the sun has been at its most intense for the last three hours, so the pond's water is

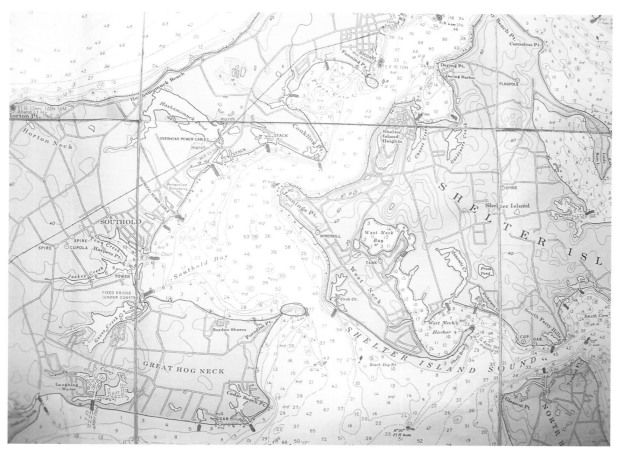

Before you start looking for tidal ponds in your boat, mark your chart where tidal outlets are shown.

A typical tidal pond's outlet at low tide.

Photograph the outlet, and mount a print on an index card listing all the data unique to that outlet.

now "hot," relatively speaking—creating ideal conditions. So scan your charts and note on your tide calendar when such a perfect day might occur. Although the perfect scenario is one that maximizes the six-hour ebb, tidal ponds can be fished successfully with fewer hours of available sunlight. The only difference is that the prime-time period is shorter.

When baitfish sense the falling tide, they begin working their way to the outlet and eventually the stream. Predator fish such as striped bass, weakfish, and fluke—those closest to the outlet—get the message first. Some may even enter the pond to find food, but for the most part, these fish are lazy (or, more accurately, bent on conserving energy). So, they lie in wait. Usually, it's only a matter of minutes before their meals are served.

Although fishing these ponds is best from late April to the end of June, depending on the latitude, you can do your tidal pond research throughout the year whenever you're on the water. If you can view a tidal pond outlet at the water's lowest point, you'll be able to see the actual exit channel without a lot of top water covering it. Always take your camera along and add to your photo gallery of the outlets in your realm. The photo should illustrate the direction of the channel exiting the

pond, how it is shaped, and where it flows. I have a set of 5- by 7-inch index cards with a photo of a pond outlet attached to one side and pertinent data on the other side, under the pond's name (if it doesn't have a name, I give it one). These photos and the accompanying information are put to good use in the spring when the fish are in.

HOW TO FISH TIDAL PONDS

After years of fishing the flats, I've discovered that what spooks fish the most is unnatural movement above and outside the water. I have watched a school of bass swim toward a boat full of motionless anglers and even pass under it. However, the slightest movement within the scope of the fish's vision can send them scurrying out of casting range. The solution is to get to the periphery of where the fish can't see you before the ebb begins flowing strongly; then keep your movements to a minimum. False casting is the fly fisher's nemesis in this situation.

When determining where to position your boat, your photo gallery of tidal pond outlets is invaluable. Using the information you've accumulated, get to the pond outlet about an hour before the ebb begins so that you can get in position before the fish arrive. For instance, if the

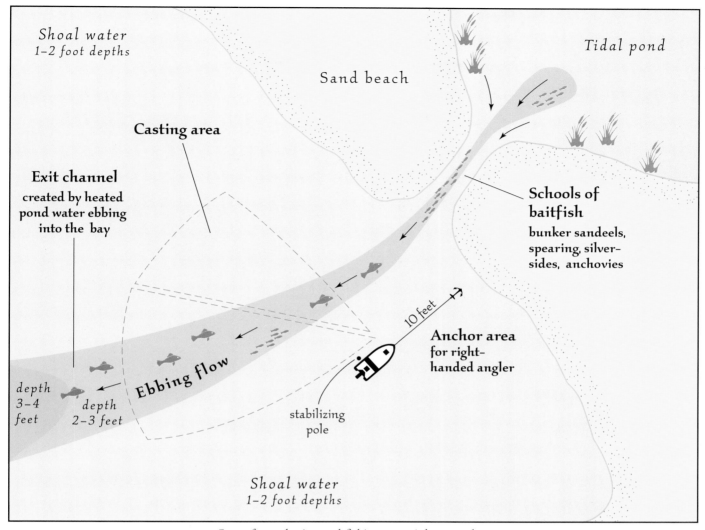

Setup for anchoring and fishing at an inlet or outlet.

anglers with me are right-handed, I slip a boat anchor into the water on the right side (facing the pond) of the pond outlet, about 10 to 15 feet from the mouth and about 10 feet to the right side on the ebbing stream. I pay out about 10 feet of line and then snub it on the bow cleat. This is sufficient, because the depth is usually only 2 or 3 feet. After the boat cocks into the tide, I have a 10-foot pole that I slip into the water on the port side of the boat, near the transom. The pole's pointed tip is buried in the mud or sand. I then fix a line from the pole to a cleat on that side of the boat. Thus, the boat is not allowed to swing into the current created by the outflow or respond to a wind that might cause it to swing on the hook and spook the fish. The boat doesn't move at all.

The angler in the bow of the boat fishes the ebbing water as if it were a trout stream. To do this effectively,

the angler casts the fly or lure over the ebbing tidal flow to the far side of the "casting area"—defined by the green lines on the accompanying drawing. The fly or lure is dropped on the far side of the stream and slightly downstream. It is then slowly retrieved across the stream as the current creates a large arc, or bow, in the line. The force of the current against the line causes the fly or lure to rise off the bottom, which is when most strikes occur.

WHEN TO MOVE ON

Not every outlet will be holding fish every time you work it. If you are still fishless after half an hour, move and head for your next tidal pond outlet. Sometimes you might have to try three or four tidal ponds before you discover where the fish have decided to dine on that particular day.

CHAPTER 13

Riding the Tide

If you're looking for camaraderie, fishing the surf is the most socially enjoyable way to catch fish. Although fishing from the beach, bridge, dock, jetty, or groin can be productive at times, it can also be quite parochial in terms of the overall fishing scene. I was a surf-casting devotee for a few years, and eventually, I could toss a lure almost out of sight. But the specter of a school of marauding striped bass or bellicose bluefish moving out of my range proved too much for me to keep my feet mired in the sand. Fish swimming beyond my reach drove me to buy my first "tin" boat. My boat buying didn't stop there, and only recently have I returned to fishing the beach.

However, it's not the same as it once was. Fishing from a boat—chasing fish instead of waiting for them to come to me—has drastically changed my approach to fishing. This is even more pronounced when I turn inward to fish the beach. One of the best ways to improve your catch of predator fish—striped bass, bluefish, weakfish, fluke, and even the occasional albacore that searches the surf for food—is to hitch a ride on the back of the tide. I've been doing this for the last dozen years and can't believe I never took advantage of it before. It's a simple idea.

During July and August, I switch my fishing activity from the broad and lengthy tidal flats between the North and South Forks of Long Island (New York) to structure fishing along the island's edges. Although structure fishing describes where I fish, I'm really fishing the mini-flats—between the beach and about 10 feet of water. In Long Island Sound, there's a tidal current moving up and down the beach, with deeper water just a dozen feet or so off the sands.

Fortunately, I live on a unique island that has a stretch of beach almost 130 miles long on its northern shore. The tidal range here averages about 6 feet, and every six hours and twenty-eight minutes it reverses its direction along the beach. The average tidal flow is about 2 knots. This means that, with a wind blowing with the tide, I could effortlessly cover about 10 miles of beach. However, I've never gotten beyond 4 or 5 miles.

The structure I fish along Long Island's North Shore was created by numerous New England boulders that were rounded and rolled a couple hundred miles to the

Top: When you utilize the tidal current, the boat drifts along the beach's mini-flats. Only slight bursts from the electric motors are needed to keep the caster facing the beach.

south by the last glacier. About 20,000 years ago, this continental ice sheet stood a mile high above what is now Manhattan and Long Island. The leading edge of the glacier was like the blade of a bulldozer. When it stopped and began to melt, it left on the beach and in the water a clutter of boulders that today looks a lot like the old French Maginot Line. This has produced bass-holding structure beyond belief. The boulders vary in size from small cannonballs to a few that are as big as an eighteen-wheeler; most, however, are about the size of the old VW Beetle. Their sides are adorned with long strands of kelp and other sea grasses whose filament-like bodies change direction with the tide. Beneath the grasses are hordes of barnacles attached to the boulders' bare areas. Lobsters—one of the striped bass's favorite foods—live under the boulders' edges. It's a veritable Garden of Eden for food fish, and the predator fish come here to dine on them.

To fish this structure efficiently from a boat takes two people—one on the rod and one at the boat's controls. The first step is to appraise the tidal situation. I fish both the flood (incoming) and the ebb (outgoing) tide, but the flood tide is usually a bit more productive. I believe that the constant reflooding of the sloping edge of the beach attracts predator fish to see whether anything new has fallen into what will soon be their domain again. If you know what these fish eat and when and where they eat it, catching them is simply a matter of interrupting that process.

To do this, I run my boat along the beach to the head of the flooding tide and then let it carry me in its flooding direction, either miles or yards, until the tide turns. When the boat begins to ride on the back of the flowing tide, I cut the engine and switch to two electric motors mounted on the transom, using them to bring me within casting distance of the beach (you can also pole the boat to the beach, but that often requires a muscle-aching effort). The boat addresses the beach at a right angle—that is, pointing right at it. The boat oper-ator's job is to keep the boat close to the beach so the angler in the bow can reach the sands with either a fly rod or a spinning outfit. In other words, the tide moves the boat up or down the beach, and the person at the controls moves it in and out. Where I fish, the water is pocked with boulders, and I'm constantly dodging them. Occasionally I might bump a boulder, but the tide's force is so gentle that no damage is done.

Surf casters who have never worked the beach from the outside won't believe all the "new" water they can cover just by letting the tide move them. And after several years of fishing this technique, I've discovered that most of the fish we catch hit the lure within 5 feet of dry sand. I have also found that poppers are the most effective plugs, but plugs with diving planes that allow the plug to follow the contour of the beach into deeper water are also very effective in enticing hungry fish in the depths. Finally, hinged or jointed plugs have a slight advantage over one-piece plugs.

When fly-fishing for bass, I use either a slow-sinking or a floating line with a sinking tip. I don't believe you have to go really deep into the structure to entice a bass. The reason is that, unlike most fish, striped bass are walleyed. In fact, bass have a bit of binocular vision and are thus able to sense depth and distance. In addition, their eyes are turned slightly upward. Because of this, they can see action on or near the surface even when they are in deep water, and it doesn't take them long to climb the 7 or 8 feet to the top. This is one reason why popping plugs on the surface are such effective striped bass baits.

One drawback to the riding-the-tide technique can be the wind. It is best employed when the wind isn't a factor or in a leeward setting. When the wind is blowing from inshore, off the land, and over the beach, it can make your maneuvering as the boat's skipper a bit challenging. This is especially so when the wind rises above 5 or 10 knots and tends to push you offshore. Here, the only solution is to switch to the other side of the island.

CHAPTER 14

Fishing in Shallow Water

Cast there!

FLY-FISHING

Fly-fishing success on the flats relies on two things: the ability to cast accurately to a designated spot, and the ability to cast at least 50 feet (whereas the average recreational angler casts only about 30 feet). Although distance is important, it's not as crucial as accuracy. Distance can be compensated for by moving the boat closer to the fish. However, if the boat gets too close, the chances of spooking the fish are drastically increased.

Spot Casting

Determining where the fly should land is based on the angler's reflexes, both mental and physical. The ability to spot the fish comes with experience, as does the ability to instantly determine in which direction it is swimming. The brain, acting with the speed of a computer, must predict the path the fish will take, based on what it has just seen. Then you must choose the appropriate place to land the fly and the fly line so as not to frighten the fish.

The two distances that must be calculated are how far in front of the fish and how far beyond its route, at right angles, the fly should land. These measurements vary according to the species of fish. Fish such as bonefish or permit are very spooky, but red drum, snook, bluefish, and fluke are more tolerant about the sky seeming to fall on them. Striped bass, weakfish, and spotted sea trout are somewhere in between these two groups. Again, experience is often the best determinant of the correct distance from and the best location in relation to the fish's snout.

In addition, you must factor in the amount of time you need to take up the slack in the line lying on top of the water as the cast ends, as well as how quickly you must begin stripping the line to put the fly and the fish on a collision course. At first, all this planning may seem impossible to accomplish, but fortunately, most of the coordination among the eyes, brain, and muscles is automatic and swift.

Blind Casting and False Casting

Although it is generally far more productive to wait and watch rather than to cast and watch, there is a role for blind casting—casting with no target in sight—when sight-fishing on the flats. After a period of slowly cruising and searching for fish, an angler may want to break the boredom and the forced immobility by making a few casts. Often, this results in a surprise. Even in clear, shallow water, predator fish can be difficult to see because of their natural camouflage. Or they may be hidden by grasses, boulders, or logs in the water. A blind cast might be enough to bring them out into view.

In addition, before going into the bucket for the first time, the angler should make a series of false casts to warm up his or her muscles, much like an athlete. When the angler feels that the rod, the line, and the muscles are all working together, the line is stripped into the bucket, and the rod is added and left there until a fish is spotted.

Loading the Line and Making the Cast

Once a fish is spotted but not yet within casting range, the rod comes out of the bucket, and a flip of the rod tip puts the fly, the leader, and whatever line is beyond the top guide onto the water on the side of the boat (the right side if the angler is right-handed). The rod tip is then pointed astern, almost against the boat's hull, and held just a foot or two above the water. While this is going on, the boat's engine has been turned off, but because of its momentum, the boat is still moving. The line is left on the water, dragging more line through the guides and from the bucket as the boat moves ahead. Ideally, all the line will be in the water by the time the boat is within casting distance of the fish.

The angler then quickly brings the rod forward, as if in a side cast, and the line in the water drags or bends and loads the rod tip. The rod now acts as if it is just recovering from a backcast. The rod is moved swiftly as if in a forward cast, and the line finally breaks free of the water. It shoots ahead as if it were cast to the spot where the fly will intercept the fish.

If the cast doesn't result in a strike, many anglers return the full length of line used in a cast to the water at boatside, even as the boat is slowly cruising over the flats. They do this because there is likely to be more than one fish in the area, and they want to be ready to make a quick cast even though the boat is moving. Casting

Although working the flats from a boat is usually easy fishing, sometimes obstructions keep you out of range, as on Moho Key in southern Belize.

directly forward in such a situation is useless, because the angler can't strip in line faster than the boat's forward movement. However, casts at angles of 90 degrees or less are effective.

If the fly doesn't land in the right spot and the fish isn't spooked, the angler hauls in the line, makes just one backcast, and redirects the fly on the forward cast. This may occur several times in quick succession as the angler tries to get the fly ahead of a fast-moving fish. There is no false-casting involved—only one backcast to keep the amount of movement in the bow of the boat to a minimum.

Roll Casting

One of the most effective ways to get the line off the water and moving forward from a stationary boat is the roll cast. It isn't used as often as it should be. It works well and doesn't require a backcast. It also works nicely as the second cast when used in conjunction with line loading using the water.

Casting to Windward

This technique is never easy, and on windy days, a switch to a heavier rod and line can make a difference. Also, switching from a floating to a slow or moderate sinking line can force it farther into the wind. Another

aid is to use flies that aren't big and fluffy and that offer less resistance. When all else fails, work areas where the wind is behind you, which can actually help with longer forward casts. The only drawback is that backcasts don't load the line as heavily as they should because you are now casting upwind.

To Strip or Not to Strip?

Movement is needed when using flies that resemble baitfish or when movement is the key to attracting a predator's interest. With certain flies, however, you don't need to strip in line to give the fly movement; in fact, movement is a hindrance. For example, when using crab patterns, the fly is cast within sight of the fish and allowed to settle naturally to the bottom. Crab flies are weighted, often to one side, so that it looks like the crab is slipping off from one side to the other as it sinks. Even if the fish doesn't strike the fly, it is left to settle into the mud or grass. Then a slight twitch or two gives the fly the look of a live crab, encouraging the fish to attack. If there is no response, strip the line in quickly and try again.

Shrimp flies can also be fished like crab flies, but in this case, the line is twitched ever so slightly as the fly descends toward the bottom. This twitching makes the fly resemble a swimming shrimp. Some anglers disregard this fact and strip the line in short bursts, which doesn't

Blind-casting the beach can pay unexpected dividends and is always worth a few tries when nothing seems to be around.

Spin casting is the most productive way to cover a large piece of the flats.

imitate a shrimp, but it does catch fish. Try it both ways to see which is more effective on the flats where you fish.

SPIN-FISHING

Spin fishing on the flats offers several advantages over fly-casting. First, as in fly fishing, accuracy is the paramount requirement for success, but in spin fishing, that accuracy is far easier to achieve. Second, spin-fishing lures, attached to light lines, cast considerably farther than the distance achievable by the majority of fly casters. That superior accuracy and distance may mean more fish for anglers, whether novice or experienced. Third, even the best spinning gear—rods, reels, lines, and lures—cost a lot less than comparable fly-fishing equipment. This means that anglers may be able to afford two or three different outfits for larger and larger fish.

However, there is a downside to spinning: the lures. In spin fishing, it is the weight of the plugs and spoons that pulls the line off the reel, and these heavy things make a bigger splash on the water than do feathery flies. Although sometimes a big, noisy splash can attract fish, most of the time it just scares them.

Spot Casting

Finding the intercept spot is easier with a spinning rod. And if you miss it, you can quickly wind in and recast the lure until you get it right. Of course, the fish might not wait around for your accuracy to improve. There is also less commotion on the bow platform when casting a spinning rod. A simple underhand cast, with a snap at the wrist, sends the lure flying. And because you can make faster casts, you are likely to catch up sooner to a fast-moving fish than with a fly rod. In addition, because of the longer casting abilities of a spinning rod, you don't have to be as close to the fish to reach it. As a fish hunter, you can adopt the attitude of a sniper with your long casts.

Casting Poppers

Spin fishing reaches its zenith when it comes to tossing small surface poppers—floating, cupped lures anywhere from 1½ to 3 inches long. You can make them dance and pop more realistically when using a spinning outfit. Small metallic spoons, with or without feathers, and small jointed swimming plugs also work well; few fish can resist this action.

CHAPTER 15

Maximizing Your Flats Fishing

Are you getting the most out of the flats you fish? If not, this chapter can help. As noted in chapter 11, a water depth of 1 to 4 feet is ideal. However, water depth is something that can be manipulated, because not all flats are created equal, and more important, not all flats are really flats. In fact, most of the flats on the Atlantic shore, north of Cape Hatteras, are anything but flat. The situation is even more evident on the West Coast.

In the Northeast, the flats are actually gradients, but the angle is so slight that most anglers don't notice the subtle but distinct incline. By changing your location on a flat, you can vary the depth of the water you fish. Even better, you can make sure that it is within the ideal of 1- to 4-foot range for your entire route on the flats.

In order to manipulate the depth of the water you fish, you must understand a few basic tidal characteristics. Tide is actually the vertical measurement of the water's depth—not the in-and-out flow of water that most peo-

ple call the "tide." The duration of a flood (incoming) tide and an ebb (outgoing) tide is, on average, a bit less than six and a half hours (not six hours, as many anglers believe). This is because the tide is measured on a lunar calendar. The moon, on its twenty-eight-day cycle, along with a little help from the sun, creates the pull on the earth's oceans that results in a tide. Also, the occurrence of slack water—when the tide is at its lowest or highest level—varies every twenty-four hours by an average of fifty minutes. For example, if the tide at the spot where you caught a big bass today was at its highest at 3 P.M., tomorrow at the same spot the maximal tide height will occur fifty minutes later, or at roughly 3:50 P.M.

In addition to this daily variation in water height, the average height of a tide grows progressively from south to north. In other words, there is almost no tide at

Top: This angler found his bass when the flat was almost devoid of tidal water.

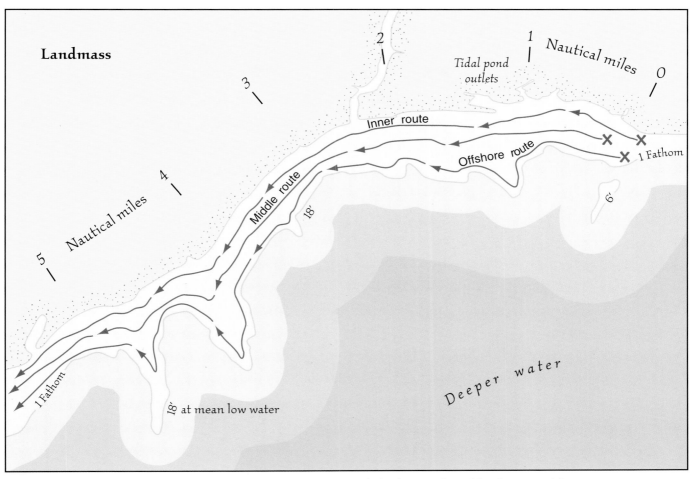

Potential routes for cruising the flats at various tide levels are indicated by the arrowed lines.

the earth's equator, but in the Bay of Fundy, tides can range up to 45 feet. The height of the tide is also affected by the direction of the wind, which can pile up the water in a bay or keep a tide from reaching its potential if the wind's blowing against the tidal flow. Another variable that affects tide height is the pull of full and new moons. Spring tides have nothing to do with the season; they are tides that take place just after a new or full moon (which occur fourteen days apart), when there is the greatest difference between high and low water. Neap tides occur just after the first or third quarter of the moon, when there is the least difference between high and low water.

How do all these factors influence your ability to maximize the coverage of a flat? I can best describe it by using one of the flats I hunt regularly as an example. This flat is ¾ to 1½ nautical miles wide and 6 nautical miles long—almost 4,000 acres of fishing possibilities (unusually large for the northeastern Atlantic coast). Its axis runs east and west, with a landmass along the entire length of its north side. Along the southern, outer edge

of this flat, the water is 3 fathoms (18 feet) deep and is unsuitable for sight fishing, as is the 2-fathom line in the middle of the flat. My fishing ground is between the 0- and 1-fathom line. Conveniently, all these artificial lines parallel the actual shape of the dry land to the north. Here, the actual fishable area varies in width from ¾ to 1¼ nautical miles—still a lot of water to cover. Intruding into the lateral course of the flats from the landmass to the north (the shoreline) are eight tidal ponds whose dredged outlet-inlet channels, with their deeper water, attract fish. The fish use them much like exits on an expressway, and these are prime fishing spots.

How can you control the depth of the flats to meet the 1- to 4-foot criterion for maximal visibility? Here, I do so by choosing one of three possible routes that parallel the beach. Determining which route to take depends on the state of the tide when I begin to cruise. If the tide is at its highest, I choose the "inside" route, the one just off the beach. Even at the lowest part of the tide, there is still 1 to 2 feet of water here, and at the highest part of tide, there can be as much as 4 feet of water along the beach.

This 31-pound bass was picked off the flats when the tide was against the beach, at it highest mark.

It is impossible to cover all 6 miles of the course's length at the slow pace demanded for spotting fish. I figure that running at 1 mile per hour is slow enough to see everything that might be a feeding fish. I always begin in the east in the morning so the sun is at my back, avoiding the reduced visibility caused by sun glare. Thus, I run this "inside" course until the falling tide progressively lowers the water to about the 2-foot mark. Bass and weakfish become increasingly more skittish as the water depth gets skinnier.

At this low-water point, I turn the boat into deep water, head beyond the 3-fathom curve, and return to near where I started. Again, this keeps the sun at my back. Then I locate the second water route on the flat that has a 3-foot depth and head west again. On rare occasions, I run the "offshore," 3-fathom route, before the tide bottoms out.

The opposite scenario comes into play when I start fishing when the tide is dead low. Then, I run just north of the 1-fathom mark, usually in about 4 feet of water, as the tide begins to rise on the inclined flat. Whatever the state of the tide, I begin on that part of the inclined flat where the water is between 2 and 3 feet deep.

Do I ever get to fish the western end of my flat? Yes I do, because each day, the starting point is about 2 miles farther west along the initial route, usually at the end of the route I finished the day before. In reality, I have tri-sected the 6-mile flat into three 2-mile sections. Thus, I fish "new" water for about 2 miles, then return and fish the next route. Using this staging technique, I fish the same stretch of water, weather permitting, only every four to six days. In all, the full course is 18 miles long. This is the way to adequately cover a flat.

CHAPTER 16

The Future of Sight Fishing

Although some aspects of sight fishing are quite old, the innovations and new directions of the last decade have produced techniques that could not have been imagined just a few years ago. Have we reached the zenith in sight fishing, or are there new vistas to seek?

FISHING GEAR AND EQUIPMENT

The rods and their component parts for fishing the flats are everything we could ask for. They are light, strong, well balanced, extremely functional, and fairly affordable. The reels are real wonders of achievement, and they almost seem to think for themselves. Fly and spinning lines have undergone tremendous changes in their design and construction, making longer casts possible and accurate casts easier. One aspect of sight fishing that will probably never stop evolving—as long as it is controlled by the human brain, mind, and hands—is the design of fly patterns.

Have we reached the ultimate in the design of flats boats? Perhaps. Right now, they seem to be as good as they can get. They float in a minimum amount of water and have three great sources of propulsion—push pole, inboard or outboard engines, and electric motors. What

more could we want? I'm sure someone will eventually find a way to build something better.

THE FISH

Fish stocks everywhere in the world are declining—some slowly, but others quite rapidly. Are the species that sight fishers chase on the flats more prone to stock losses than others? Because many flats species are not really edible, there might be a bit of salvation there. But what about those fish that are culinary delights? With the saving of the redfish, we saw what organized pressure from recreational anglers can achieve. We have also seen juvenile pompano return to the flats, but where they have no management protection, they are still threatened.

When a fish is officially designated a gamefish, it is given a special status that protects it from commercial interests. This protection comes in the form of seasons as well as bag and length limits. State or federal agencies are responsible for fish management, and these efforts are often supported by fishing license fees. Striped bass anglers have fought for more than fifty years to make it a gamefish, and this status has been granted in many

Top: Does catch-and-release really work?

coastal states. Elsewhere, however, the fish is so valuable commercially that special-interest lobbying groups have been able to thwart gamefish status. Thus, in several states where striped bass spawn, they can still be caught and sold.

CATCH-AND-RELEASE

Can catch-and-release be a solution to the decline of fish stocks? It might be part of the solution, but it won't work by itself. From a biologist's point of view, catch-and-release might be feasible, given the right ambient water temperature and the right time factor. But as noted in chapter 8, this would require a change in our basic sportfishing ethic, which now espouses two diametrically opposed ideas. On the one hand, it states that sportsmen should give fish a fighting chance, choosing equipment that pits an angler's ability against a fish's desire to live. And the outcome of that battle should never be predetermined by the size and kind of fishing equipment used. On the other hand, it expresses a self-serving desire that the fish be permitted to live to fight another day. Yet the longer it takes to catch and release a fish (using "sporting" equipment), the poorer its chance of survival. For catch-and-release to result in live fish, we would have to use "nonsporting" equipment to quickly overpower the fish.

Will anglers adopt the requisite new ethic? I doubt it. In reality, catch-and-release is just a misguided justification for using light tackle. The only genuine justification for light tackle is if you intend to catch and then kill the fish for your table. But how many fish can you eat?

HABITAT DEGRADATION

There is no question that habitat degradation is a problem. During the great suburban housing boom after World War II, millions of acres of tidal wetlands from Boston to Baltimore were filled in and developed. Unfortunately, this land can't be reclaimed, and the best that we can hope for is to stop additional losses. Building along such wetlands is now tightly controlled by both federal and state agencies. However, habitat loss has already caused the near extinction of a dozen or more species—including sheepshead, lafayette, smelt, croaker, drum, whiting, kingfish, blowfish, and winter flounder—that once used the tidal marshes as nurseries.

Though history may be prologue to the future, human beings' incessant demand for space and the good life have caused them to forget the past. The same kind of suburban expansion that took place fifty years ago in the Northeast is now running rampant along the coast from Virginia to Texas. Restrictive regulations in many of these coastal states have only slowed the land filling and the beachfront construction, as developers have found ways to circumvent these constraints.

INDEX